KU-735-900

Acknowledgements

Some of the material in this book has appeared elsewhere, sometimes in slightly different versions. I would like to thank the editors and publishers of *Media, Culture & Society*; UNESCO's Division of Cultural Development; NACLA's *Latin American Report*; Bergin and Garvey, publishers of June Nash and Helen Safa's *Sex and Class in Latin America*; International General Editions, publishers of A. Mattelart and Seth Siegelaub's *Communication and Class Struggle*.

I am also grateful to the French editors of *Les Temps Modernes*; *Tel Quel*; *Cahiers de Recherche de Sciences de Textes, Université Paris 7*.

Crispin Aubrey contributed editing suggestions at several points. I would like to thank for their translation, Mary C. Axtmann (Part Two, 2), David Buxton (Part Three, 1 and 3) and Keith Reader (Part One).

On a more personal level, I am infinitely grateful to Armand for the constant dialogue.

M.M.

About the author

Michèle Mattelart was born in France, on the coast of Brittany.

In 1963, having completed her studies in comparative literature and sociology, she left for Latin America, Chile, where she lived until 1973. After the *coup d'état* which brought an end to the government of Popular Unity on 11 September, 1973, Michèle Mattelart returned to Paris although she remains closely linked to Latin America and visits frequently.

Michèle Mattelart began her research into culture and communication in Chile, specialising in the relationship between women, politics and the media. In Santiago she worked at the Centre for Research into National Reality which was founded at the University of Chile but closed down by the military the day after the *coup d'état*.

Apart from her research work and teaching during the period of the government of Popular Unity, she took up a post in the programming department of the Chile National television station (Channel 7). She was also involved in the "Editorial Quimantu" and influential in launching the youth magazine *Onda*.

Back in France she continued her research. Married to Armand Mattelart, with whom she has written numerous works, she has two sons – Tristan and Gurvan – both born in Chile.

Michèle Mattelart has just finished editing, with Armand Mattelart, a book on the new paradigms of critical theory of communication. (*Thinking of media, elements of a critical theory of communication*.)

Michèle Mattelart has published the following works: *La mujer chilena en una nueva sociedad* (The Chilean Woman in a New Society), Editorial del Pacifico, Santiago, Chile, 1968. *La ideologia de la prensa liberal en Chile* (The Ideology of the liberal press in Chile), *Cuadernos de la realidad nacional*, Santiago, 1970, in collaboration with A. Mattelart and M. Piccini; *La cultura de la opresion femenina* (The culture of feminine oppression), Editorial Era, Mexico, 1977; *De l'usage des medias en temps de crise* (On the use of the media in times of crisis), A. Moreau, Paris, 1979, in collaboration with A. Mattelart; *International Image markets*, Comedia, London, 1984, with A. Mattelart and X. Delcourt. She is also author of numerous articles, notably in English. "Education, Television and Mass Culture: reflections on research into innovation" in *Television in Transition*, BFI Publishing, London, 1985.

Comedia Series ● 33

WOMEN, MEDIA AND CRISIS

FEMININITY AND DISORDER

Michèle Mattelart

Comedia Publishing Group
9 Poland Street, London W1V 3DG   Tel: 01-439 2059

Comedia Publishing Group was set up to investigate and monitor the media in Britain and abroad. The aim of the project is to provide basic information, investigate problem areas, and to share the experiences of those working in the field, while encouraging debate about the future development of the media. The opinions expressed in the books in the Comedia series are those of the authors, and do not necessarily reflect the views of Comedia. For a list of other Comedia titles see back pages.

First published in 1986 by Comedia Publishing Group
9 Poland Street, London W1V 3DG

British Library Cataloguing in Publication Data
Mattelart, Michèle
Women, media, crisis: femininity and disorder
1.   Women – social conditions
I.   Title
305.4'2   HQ1206

ISBN 0-906890-96-9

Cover Design by Richard Doust

Typeset by Photosetting, 6 Foundry House, Yeovil, Somerset BA20 1NL. (0935) 23684

Printed in Great Britain by Unwin Brothers Ltd., Gresham Press, Old Woking, Surrey

Trade Distribution by George Philips, Arndale Road, Lineside Industrial Estate, Littlehampton, West Sussex

Contents

Foreword

The new self-awareness of women, and the women's movements which have developed over the last twenty years, have had a considerable destabilising effect on the sexual distribution of roles – one of the principal foundations of society. Even if these movements do not embrace all women of all social groups or classes, they have still established a new, alternative and conflicting point of reference.

This change in the image and role of women has been endorsed and encouraged to a certain extent by an economic system which has profited from it in times of expansion. Magazines and media programmes specially aimed at women have adjusted themselves to this new market and have even accepted the problems and conflicts arising from this new image of women as suitable subject matter for their products.

Crises always threaten to usher in a revival of the philosophies of security. This is true at an individual, domestic and national level, as well as internationally. The present economic crisis is accompanied by a moral crisis to which women have greatly contributed. In my opinion, this is probably one of the most important aspects of the contemporary global crisis. And this in turn invites us to focus on a decisive issue: the present crisis has to find a solution to a number of specific contradictions which arise from the unrest among women, to whom – because of their restricted autonomy – the ruling culture has assigned a regulatory or pacifying role, and responsibility for maintaining a balance in society.

So it is important to ask what image of women does the media naturally promote? And what change occurs in the universe of symbols during periods of crisis, as compared with times of relative stability? These are two of the fundamental questions which this collection of essays tries to answer.

In liberal democracies, the legitimacy of the culture of "modernity" is closely linked to the ability of the economic and political order to respond to democratisation by the market and to the ever-increasing consumption of goods and services. The seduction of the world of material goods, which is widely associated in modernist ideology with the idea of a female being, is based on an overemphasis on growth. What happens in times of recession, when the economy comes into conflict with its own dynamic of stimulating the desire for growth and well-being?

This is my first approach to the theme of "women and the media", an attempt to elucidate or analyse continuities and ruptures in the way in which the symbolic order processes the relationship between femininity and modernity in normal times, and in times of crisis.

In times of crisis, the theme of the family once again comes to the fore. By contrast with the difficulties experienced in the external world, by contrast with the threats to employment and to purchasing power, the family appears as a haven of safety and refuge. The cultural industries, by the way in which they manage crisis themes, effectively encourage this movement back to the family unit. In the advanced industrial countries, this movement is also encouraged by politics designed to raise the birth rate (in some European countries, increased benefits are payable on the birth of the third child), by moral "regeneration" policies (anti-abortion campaigns in Ronald Reagan's America), and by fiscal penalties against households in which both the father and the mother are breadwinners. Behind all these measures looms the threat which the crisis represents for women's jobs, since women are often the first victims of both unemployment and manpower cuts. In times of crisis, the idea of women as "job-snatchers" also recovers all its latent potency.

Some historians take the view that the closed, nuclear family – an inheritance from the early years of the twentieth century – has been shaken but not undermined over the past two decades, and that the crisis has had the effect not of loosening, but strengthening, family solidarity. This strengthening of family solidarity is perfectly in keeping with the new requirements for survival which have been created by the redefinition of the liberal state, since the restructuring of power – the latent historical consequence both of the crisis and of the evolution of liberal economies – is in many countries a challenge to the survival of the Welfare State. The gradual disintegration of this type of state, which protects the working classes against excessive social inequalities, leads to a strengthening of family ties as a spontaneous reaction of self-defence. Now that the Welfare State is in crisis, the new power structure – with its distinctly élitist bias in favour of individual and private initiative, and with its justification of open and unrestricted competition – is seeking to delegate to the family some of the responsibilities it held towards the community. So the family becomes the arena for different types of personal and social relations.

My second theme in this collection is more closely linked with my living political experience in Latin America, more precisely in popular Chile between 1970 and 1973. During those years in Chile I came to feel how paradoxical is the very idea of femininity, torn between order and disorder, in the context of a revolutionary crisis. There are certain latent values in the concept of "femininity" which help to reproduce the established order in times of peace, and which can be reactivated in periods of disruption, when the ruling interests are threatened. In these political situations, conservative forces are able to reap the rewards of the ideological investments they have made through the various institutions which take part in the socialisation of women. The women of the Chilean conservative forces played a decisive role in the ideological preparation for the fascist coup d'état in September 1973. The Right flung into the fray the counter-revolutionary capacity of its female supporters – transformed into a mass army of activists.

The Right also made use of women on this occasion by according them the status of *public representatives* in addition to the *private status* in which it usually confines women, and relying on the image of woman as mother and housewife to justify her behaviour as "natural" and non-political. And once again, using this stereotype of femininity in which women are weak and – like children – need a father, an offensive tactic of a deliberately sexual nature was formulated. Through this, the power of the state was equated with the power of the male, and the military was regarded in this crisis situation as the best answer to the need for a virile state. In their opposition to the authority "of the people", regarded as a usurper and synonymous with chaos, women appealed directly to the principle of authority, synonymous with order, which gives the strong state its justification as being "man's business".

The essays in this book were written between 1971 and 1982. Some of them were originally written in Spanish in Chile (*The myth of modernity*, 1971; *The media and revolutionary crisis*, 1972). *The feminine side of the coup*, 1973–1974, was written, in the months following my expulsion from Santiago, in France, as well as *Giving birth to the gun*, written in Paris during 1977. Both were written originally in French. The other essays included here were produced in 1981 or early 1982, in French. It is the first time that these essays have been brought together in any language. Some of them have been published separately in English in journals, reviews or anthologies. Others appear in English for the first time.

This volume recognises *the crisis* as paradigm, and this idea serves to highlight the unity of these essays. It represents the Ariadne's thread intertwining the analysis of femininity both in normal times and in times of disruption. In doing so, it perhaps avoids the trap of a binary approach to the dilemma. Doesn't disorder reveal more of the workings of femininity than order? For that reason, the essays reproduced here do not necessarily appear in the chronological order of their production.

These essays bear the hallmark of the era in which they were written – both in terms of the theoretical approach and actual concepts used.

Since 1982 I have been very much concerned to "return to the subject", and therefore to follow up the ideas first formulated in these essays on the analysis of the female consumer and the interaction between the subjective feminine sense of time and certain "popular" consumer products. My present research is based on this theoretical perspective. If I have thought it worthwhile to make these essays once again available (some of which originally appeared over fifteen years ago), it is because by doing so I hope to provide a better understanding of the origins of a particular approach.

I dedicate this book to the women and men of Latin America with whom I shared a deep friendship and who paid with their lives for the passion with which they lived – without always being clearly conscious that these were decisive moments through which was being formed, ultimately, our liberation.

Michèle Mattelart
Paris, April 1985

Part One

Everyday life

1: From soap to serial: the media and women's reality

An episode from the 1920s – in other words, right at the beginning of that important technological medium that radio was to become – provides a good illustration of the close link between symbolic mass-production and the production of material goods in the nascent industrial society of the United States. At the same time, it shows us how women were straightaway singled out, from this commercial point of view, to become the favourite target for mass media messages, an essential factor in the planning of programmes.

Glen Sample worked at the time for a small advertising agency (later to become in the 1960s Dancer, Fitzgerald and Sample). He was the first person to adapt for radio a serial that had appeared in a newspaper – "The married life of Helen and Warren". On the air this became "Betty and Bob" and was sponsored by the well known flour brand Gold Metal, at the time manufactured by the firm Washburn Grosby and Co., later to become General Mills.

Shortly afterwards, Mr Sample turned his attention to Oxydol washing powder. The manufacturers, Procter and Gamble, were then on the point of going to the wall under the attack of the English Company, Unilever, which had successfully launched the brand Rinso. Massively plugged by Mr Sample's radio serials and the advertising that interrupted them, Oxydol triumphed over Rinso. The serial, called "Ma Perkins", whose career on the air went on and on for almost thirty years, gave Oxydol the decisive impetus.[1] "Soap opera", the radio (and subsequently television) version of the "lonely hearts" press, was born.

The name given to the new genre is as interesting as it is unusual. Isn't it unprecedented for a cultural product to indicate so crudely its material origin (here linked to the sale of soap and detergent) and its conscription in the battle between different commercial brands? At the same time, a whole *household* definition of a broadcast literature reveals itself plainly, making unambiguously clear a twofold function: to promote the sale of household products, and to subsume the housewife in her role by offering her romantic gratification.

Only much later did the feminine factor come to be important in the programming of European radio stations, notably in France. In fact, French radio did not start as a public service. There were state stations before the war, but they co-existed with private ones. Advertising certainly existed, but not (as in the same period in the United States) as the norm around which programming was structured.[2] It usually came in only as a subsidy for cultural programmes (often concerts), which were also supported by groups of listeners. We can therefore observe a certain continuity between the classic forms of cultural life (concerts, plays, shows put on by local associations, etc.) and the programming of these radio stations. The history of television was likewise marked by the same preponderance of classic culture – plays, films and concerts – rather than a specifically televisual genre.

These radio programmes included, in the morning, "Women's Hour" (the day's menu, recipes, etc.), but overall the programming, whose high spot was undoubtedly the news, was made up essentially of rebroadcast concerts, cultural and scientific broadcasts, radio plays and entertainment programmes like quiz games – all types of programme which do not immediately segregate their audience by sex.

After World War II, when so-called "peripheral" radio stations made their appearance, escaping the previous state monopoly on broadcasting, the commercial model became dominant. And this model was progressively to acknowledge the tremendous importance of the mass female public.

Radio Luxembourg came into existence in 1933 with the lofty aim of "acquainting listeners in different countries with the artistic and cultural masterpieces of the whole world". In 1935, it introduced "L'heure des dames et des demoiselles" ("Women's Hour"), which became a feminine byword and continued right through to 1966. In 1935, the introduction of radio serials coincided with the beginnings of a wider development of programming: as with all private radio stations, entertainment began to nibble away the air-time hitherto reserved for classical music. Regularly, radio games, weekly radio plays, and the "hurly-burly of the music hall" (sponsored by Cadoricin Lotion) made their appearance. From 1955, Europe-1 and Radio Luxembourg (now RTL – Radio Television Luxembourg) competed vigorously through radio serials. To Europe's serial, RTL responded with "Nicole et l'amour" (Nicole and Love). It was also in competition with RTL that Europe-1 introduced Ménie Grégorie's well known programmes of advice on sexuality and family psychology.[3]

RTL rapidly multiplied its claims to be the leading commercial radio station. The first multinational radio station in Europe, it was also the first to broadcast throughout the day. In 1977, this same station calmly admitted that advertising could account for twenty per cent of its air-time, that most of its public was female, and that these considerations laid down certain lines of programming. "Women's attitude towards radio is significant: what they fundamentally want is somebody there... RTL will therefore fill this space and accompany our listener with its voice, in her home, *in her everyday life*" (author's italics).

Everyday life. Day-to-day life. These phrases represent a specific idea of time within which women's social and economic rôle is carried out. It is in the everyday time of domestic life that the fundamental discrimination of sex rôles is expressed, the separation between public and private, production and reproduction. The sphere of public interests and production is assigned to man, that of private life and reproduction to woman. The hierarchy of values finds expression through the positive value attached to masculine time (defined by action, change and history) and the negative value attached to feminine time which, for all its potential richness, is implicitly discriminated against in our society, internalised and experienced as the time of banal everyday life, repetition and monotony.

Invisible work

For a few years now, the international feminist movement, with the aid of analytical work by specialists in social science (male and female), has been vigorously denouncing the negative value attached to women's household work. This becomes transparently obvious when we think that it has always been assumed that this work should be unpaid. Now, "as a rule, once manual work is paid, it takes on economic value, so that any unpaid work (such as women's housework) becomes economically, and thus also socially and culturally, devalued".[4]

The part played by this *invisible work* in the functioning of economies has been amply demonstrated. Everywhere, in developed and developing countries alike, women form the mainstay of the *support economy* which makes it possible for all the other activities to be carried on. A woman at home performs a fundamental rôle in any economy: she services the labour force each day. This economic activity, carried on by most layers of the female population, is of great importance; but the indicators by which the socio-economic position of each country is defined, and its development measured, conceal the economic value of household work.

The arrival of capitalism, which introduced the factory and institutionalised the sale of labour power, undoubtedly represented a decisive moment in the segregation of sex rôles in the productive process, mainly by depriving the family of its old function as a productive unit. But we should beware of a nostalgic attitude, and of the tendency to idealise the situation that traditional society gave women in productive activities. It has been shown (with reference to Africa, for example), that this often went hand in hand with forms of slavery. Capitalism merely continued and deepened a hierarchical division of labour which had come into being long before, reserving for males the most prestigious and best-rewarded work and restricting women to the lowest kind. This sex rôle discrimination is fundamental to the maintenance of the capitalist economy, and it has been shown that

"but for this vast female underpinning – the women who provide food and clothing for the proletariat in a world where the necessary facilities for a collective restoration of labour energy simply do not exist – the hours of surplus value extorted from the worker by capital would be fewer. We can even say that women's work in the home is expressed through men's work outside by the creation of surplus value."[5]

Gradually isolated from the world of production through the long process of consolidation of the monogamous family and its close links with the system of private property, women, by virtue of the kind of tasks they carry out at home and their dependence on men, become the cement of class society. This division of labour finds expression in a definition of masculine and feminine qualities transmitted, reinforced and rearticulated by the different institutions of society (the Church, schools, the media). Girls will be docile, submissive, clean, chaste, prudish; they will play quiet games and enjoy indoor activities. Conversely, boys will be sexually aggressive, prone to show off their physical strength, encouraged to develop their "innate" sense of leadership, and so forth.

The invisibility of women's work and the concealment of the productive value of their household tasks are of decisive importance in determining the image of women projected by the media and the media's relationship with them. The media have made a point of following the traditional household timetable. Radio and television programming is particularly revealing in this respect: it punctuates the day with moments that make women's condition "all worth while", and helps to compensate for being shut up at home all day. It makes women's work legitimate, not as work, but as a duty (sometimes pleasurable) that *forms part of their natural function.*

The genre of these women's broadcasts may differ (afternoon magazines, television serials, radio serials); the values around which their themes are structured can correspond to different points in women's relation to capital, and to the more or less modern and free-thinking character of the sections of the bourgeoisie that produce them. But they still have in common the purpose of integrating women into their everyday life.

The exception confirms the rule – adventure consecrates routine

In this process of integration, the melodramatic serial, whether on radio or television, has traditionally played a crucial part. The serial can take several different forms and has several different tendencies, which it is not our job to analyse here. Suffice to say that most serials take as their target the family audience. But the melodramatic serial, which carries on in radio and television where "lonely hearts" columns leave off, addresses primarily the working-class female public. Because of the immense impact of this genre in Latin America and other Catholic countries, there is a tendency to think of it as a Latin genre. Yet we can see that it exists, with variations, on the screens and the air-waves of every country in the world – at least the capitalist part.

It is all too well known that the more a channel declares itself to be fulfilling a cultural function and/or that of a public service, the fewer serials it will broadcast; and this is even more true of melodramatic serials. On the other hand, they are ubiquitous on commercial channels. The profile of their audience, and their inherent regularity, make them excellent terrain for advertisers. In one hour of these serials in Venezuela, for example, there are twenty minutes of advertising. It has also been noted that there is a close link between the kind of products advertised and the subject of the day's episode.

In Latin America, undoubtedly the major territory for this genre (known there as *Telenovela*), the state channels – insignificant compared with the commercial ones, attracting only ten per cent of the audience – have tried to win over viewers by making the serials more "up-market". Major authors of contemporary Latin American literature (Salvador Garmendia in Venezuela, Gabriel Garcia Marquez in Colombia, Jorge Amado in Brazil) have been invited to contribute to this strategy, opposing to the commercial model of the dominant channels the alternative of "cultural television". There is no doubt that the results of this collaboration offer female audiences (and others) the chance to encounter cultural products with a much richer and more complex approach to human experience and emotion. But are we still talking about melodramatic serials or "telenovelas"?

The production systems currently prevalent in commercial Latin American broadcasting companies encourage directors to keep costs down and profits up by sticking to the rules of serialisation. Shooting time is minimal: the script for the following day's episode is improvised from one day to the next within the basic formulae of these mass-produced artefacts. This "on-the-spot" shooting makes it possible to take into account some social and even political issues, as well as the reactions of the public and comments by critics; but the stereotyped structure of these products, channelling the serial through a set of hackneyed recipes, reduces the effective possibilities for openness. The rules of commercialism, whose first principle is to mine the same vein to exhaustion, means that these stories go on and on interminably. The Venezuelan government had to limit the number of episodes by law.

There is no denying, however, that the interplay in a particular country between cultural channels (even in a minority) and commercial ones, can lead the latter to modify their programming, especially when they realise that the new "cultural serials" attract large audiences. Even so, in the current circumstances, these serials, like the "lonely hearts" press, remain dominated by a principle of segregation of audiences. That is the key to the matter. This genre conforms to the principle of market division that governs the culture industry. In the press, to refer to socially distinct targets (from the standpoint of both purchasing and cultural power), publishers speak of "upmarket" and "downmarket". In the field of television, the melodramatic serial indisputably belongs in the second category. And this duality of the female market increasingly pervades the whole mass cultural apparatus (a process of market democratisation and segregation at the same time).

This segregation of female audiences is so marked that the international distribution of photo novels (for example) is carried out by firms which can certainly be described as transnational, although their position nonetheless remains marginal compared to the largest multinational publishers. This market is dominated by Italian and Spanish companies and, to a lesser extent, French companies with Italian connections,[6] along with companies based in Miami, but actually the inheritors of exiled businesses that were already flourishing in Batista's Cuba. One example is the De Armas group, at the head of a real "lonely hearts" empire, which at the same time transmits transnational power in Latin America and acts as the Latin American distributor there for the Spanish versions of magazines such as *Good Housekeeping* and *Cosmopolitan*. It also publishes an international women's magazine for the Latin American market,

Vanidades.[7] (It is worth noting that Cuba was among the pioneers of the radio serial, right from the 1930s, and exported it to other Latin American countries.)

Only in June, 1978, under the titles *Kiss* and *Darling*, did the so-called "photo-novel magazines" make their appearance in the United States, in supermarkets and drugstores. As *Advertising Age* announced: "*Kiss* and *Darling* mark the first American attempt at photo-novels, a form exceedingly popular in Europe. Photo-novel magazines are similar to comic books, except that, instead of drawings, the panels contain photos of people with dialogue balloons inserted above their heads." Establishing continuity between this genre and "Mills and Boon"-style literature, these magazines are aimed at the women who read the "Harlequin" collection – Harlequin is a large multinational publisher of sentimental literature, whose parent company is based in Canada. Its French offshoot, which has operated from Paris since 1978, sold in 1980 between seventeen million and twenty-five million copies of this collection, "which carries you off into a wonderful world whose one and only dazzling heroine will be *YOU*". It publishes eighteen titles per month, 140 per year.[8] These figures certainly carry us off into a fabulous dream-world.

Today, the international distribution of television serials is the province of independent Latin American firms, who are greatly helped by the existence of a large Spanish-speaking market in the United States. This international distribution is sometimes reflected in international production, or at least script-writing. Spanish-speaking inhabitants of Miami are thus persuaded to lend a hand. This expansion has up to now taken place primarily in the United States, Central and South America and the Caribbean. It has now got as far as the Arab countries (notably Saudi Arabia) and, via Brazil, those African countries which were once Portuguese possessions. European countries, such as Spain and Portugal, are also fertile territory. In 1979, according to figures from Televisa (the monopoly Mexican commercial television station), Mexico exported 24,000 programme-hours per year of programmes and serials to the United States, Central and South America, the Caribbean and now Arab countries as well.

It is easier to grasp the size of this figure if we bear in mind that (according to a classic UNESCO study of 1972) neither French nor British television exported more than 20,000 programme-hours in that year.[9] North American television in the same period was exporting anything from 100,000 to 200,000 programme-hours and, at the time, Mexico exported only 6,000 hours at the most. Its expansion is now in full flight. The infiltration of the United States by

Mexican television has caused friction between the two countries. The firm Univision, controlled by Televisa, had made it possible, thanks to the satellite Westar, to receive Televisa programmes directly in New York and Los Angeles, whence they are channelled to the rest of the United States. This meant that by the end of 1976 more than thirteen million households watched Televisa in the United States. While nowhere near so large as the Mexican industry, Venezuela is also launching an attack on the international market. Between 1975 and 1977, twenty-three "oil serials", as they are known, were exported to North and South America, Spain, Portugal and Saudi Arabia.

It remains true that the melodramatic serial on radio or television is the fictional genre most clearly addressed to a mass female public. These productions usually have a woman's name as their title – *Natacha, Simplemente Maria, Rafaela* or whatever – a strategy which has proved successful: those serials whose titles included men's names had less of an impact. In Latin American countries, these productions continue to exist side by side with imported series (generally North American), or more up-to-date programmes which deal with the industrialised world and reflect the relative emancipation of women participating in professional life on an equal footing with men. But the traditional productions still enjoy more success. It is through these serials that the principal audience battle between the different stations is fought out.

There have been enough content analyses and ideological readings of melodramatic serials and linked genres (such as photo-novels) for us to feel able to give a highly condensed summary here.[10] The plot generally revolves round the ups and downs of a love affair which brings together people separated by social class (or age, or previous ties, or a combination of all three). The family context tends to be riddled haphazardly with social pathology and individual problems – unhappy homes, incurable diseases, illegitimate children, alcoholism, incestuous or quasi-incestuous cohabitation. The variations run the whole gamut from romantic adventures to social dramas. In Latin America, the serials are very much marked by sex and violence, obsessively present (though always shrouded in implication and innuendo) in the form of blackmail or rape. The unrolling of the story through all kinds of ambiguities, avowals, mistaken identities and interventions by a *deus ex machina* reveals a highly normative message: the good and the virtuous are rewarded. Love sanctioned by the legitimate union of marriage is better than passion, which is always punished by fate. The female characters ennoble the values of purity and virginity for girls, and often become heroic martyrs to men who in fact get away with abusing their masculine authority and class power; but, after putting her through great suffering and temptation, they confirm the happiness of the girl from a modest background by offering her a ring and married life. The sacrifice, courage, and self-denial of wives and mothers are other attitudes reinforced by these messages, crowned as they are by the return of the husband, the renewed gratitude of the son, or the simple satisfaction that comes from doing one's duty.

Monotony is countered by exceptions. The serial makes possible a symbolic revenge on the triviality of everyday life, whose monotonous repetition is countered by the day-by-day episodes of the heroine's unusual adventures. Household work, experienced as unproductive and of low socio-economic standing, is countered by programmes which give value to the area of private life and a female world dominated by "love" and "emotion".

Even before 1917, Alexandra Kollontaï, writing about the social basis of the female question, observed how very far from innocent love stories were, and how the realm of private life had been sedulously infiltrated by bourgeois standards: "Even that bourgeoisie that proclaimed love to be a 'private matter' knew how to use its moral guidelines to channel love in the direction that best suited its class interests".[11]

The greatest of the repressions carried out by what we have elsewhere called "the order of the heart" – the order that governs the organisation of this kind of melodramatic discourse – is that it invalidates any form of struggle against social inequalities (the existence of which is admitted) by means of this diffuse explanation: only love can cross class barriers. Not only is the solution individual – never collective – it is also linked to the miracle of love. Love comes to be a universal explanation which can resolve social contradictions through denying them, for the order of society, like love, is founded on Fate. The repressive order of the heart has two helpmates: Nature and Fate.

But we can notice that from the "content" point of view a tendency to increase the realism of these discourses brings them closer to the real situations of working and poor people. These new serials, at any rate in Venezuela and much more in Brazil, show an increasing concern to stick to real life. Let us look at once such example, and observe the manner in which it continues to smooth over points of conflict. The Venezuelan serial "Dona Juana" explictly refers to a problem that affects all social strata, but principally working people, and implacably brings out the sexist character of society – that of irresponsible paternity, of illegitimate children brought up by their mother alone and not recognized by the father, who abandons the mother after making her pregnant. "Dona

Juana" portrays these women, and their brave struggle against male hostility and fecklessness. But Dona Juana, of humble background, does not learn to define herself as an independent individual, even though her struggle shows the strength and energy she can display as head of the family. The *dénouement* still follows a conservative and conventional pattern: thanks to an almost miraculous stroke of luck, the father finds his daughter and recognises her. He thereby satisfies simultaneously the mother's dream and that of the daughter – that the child can bear its father's name and thus escape the stigma of illegitimacy.

It is no secret that the ideological function of these narrative discourses rests primarily in the fact that they are given as representations of reality, and therefore cling to certain features of the reality of social and class conflict, which they implicitly explain (through the mechanisms of the story) from a certain point of view, itself likewise linked to the objective reality of class struggle. The serial's twin task – of representing reality and explaining it – defines its rôle of reproducing the conditions of production of the social system, predisposing women to accept the "natural" explanation of their domination.

2: Women as consumers

One recent important strand in the theory of media studies has been a rejection of the inevitably passive way in which people react to the messages addressed at them. What is questioned is the act of consumption itself, the process by which a subject receives and appropriates. This means that the monolithic nature of the ideological effect of domination is likewise questioned. For that is the key problem. The media transmit a set of values corresponding to the interests of a particular power system. Can we infer that the recipients, reacting to the signals like Pavlov's dogs, internalise these structures of domination once and for all?

The spotlight is turned, in other words, on the act of looking and consuming: what is the relationship between the message and the subject that receives it within a personal history, or the history of a group or class? Oddly enough, there are a great many studies of media power structures, national and international, and a great many, too, of the content of media messages, but very few on the manner in which the "dominated" groups and individuals read and respond to them, or resist them (if need be through a diversion of the original intention, implicit or explicit) in the name of some ideas of their own.

Our study of the Popular Unity régime in Chile led us to try to ascertain if that historical moment, characterised by intensified social confrontations and a mobilisation of popular consciousness, led to a critical attitude towards such messages as the melodramatic serials which continued to appear on television, just as in the past. In the most active strata of working-class women, we discovered that these messages were not necessarily read as their senders intended, and that the way in which they were received denied their internal logic, leading to a roundabout process of consumption. These demystifications, particularly of the illusory social mobility often presented in the serials, emerged in comments such as the following:

"The lovers in these serials are always from a wealthy family, or a well-heeled profession, never workmen. The working class always appear as servants, or else in the character of a girl who, thanks to some miraculous encounter, becomes a great lady overnight.

Perhaps episodes can occur in real life like those depicted in these serials, but at what cost? In real life one cannot become rich without exploiting somebody else, and the serials show that the road to riches is an easy one. At whose expense do these young men and women make their wealth? It all goes to give the working class false hopes."[1]

What is disturbing, however, is the fact that these stories still provide *pleasure* for women viewers who are critically aware of how alienating they are and who have located the mechanisms through which their work is carried on. We cannot simply ignore the appeal and the pleasure (however bitter-sweet it may be when it goes hand in hand with a social and political awareness) produced by these fictional products of the cultural industry. There *is* a problem here, and one hitherto scarcely tackled. As an initial approach to it, we shall merely put forward some hypotheses about women's expectations and exhilaration.

We shall refer later to the "temporality" of women (see Part Two, *The myth of modernity*). We should recognise that the mythical hostility between the notion of women and that of change goes back to the association between the image of femininity, and of permanence and the concept of fertility. The image of woman is linked with the idea of continuation, perpetuation, duration. To the time-scale of disruption and crisis can be contrasted the female time-scale – a fluid perception of time, inhabited by eternal functions.

This specific inflection given by femininity to time can be defined as simultaneously *repetition* and *eternity*: the return of the same, eternal recurrence, the return of the cycle that links it into cosmic time, the occasion for unparallelled ecstasy in unison with the rhythm of nature, and along with that the infinite, womb-like dimension, the myth of permanence and duration.

It was this notion of a specifically female idea of time that led us to formulate the hypothesis that, above and beyond their themes and images forever retracing the dominant ideology, these lengthy stories, unfolding over protracted periods in regular daily consignments, might have much in common with this experience of repetition and eternity. These tales could well correspond to the psychic structures of women not caught up in a forward-looking idea of time, a time of change. These vast stories, delivered in daily instalments and repeated daily, would then serve, through their stereotyped rhythms, to satisfy the expectations of female subjective time. By cultivating the enjoyment of this non-forward-looking sense of time, these stories would tend to hinder women's access to the time of history, the time of project.

We shall need to check this hypothesis in the light of recent scientific researches in the field of subjectivity and the unconscious structures of personality. But what is certain is that hitherto we have been too satisfied with looking for the alienating quality of the products of the culture industry merely in the arrangement of image and word. For what continues to pose a problem, as we said earlier, is the fascination these products still exercise over spectators (of either sex) who are perfectly capable of giving an acute analysis of the serials' alienating characteristics. What collective masochism, what suicidal group-attitude can explain this fascination?

One theory is that the power of the culture industry is also to be found outside the subjects with which it deals, the anecdotes it transmits, which are but foreshadows of its real message. What is not said would then count for more than what is said. Does the culture industry not restore the psychic patterns of the mass of people, patterns which are elements of nature as well as of culture? Could its ideological function not also be fulfilled in this constant restimulation of the deep structures of a collective unconscious? The crucial importance of the question in terms of formal or informal strategies for resistance should be plain. One complement to the basic development of self-awareness should surely be the need to sound out the "group unconscious".

We cannot leave the problem here. We have to see what these questions can contribute to the construction of an alternative, and how we can give a *non-alienated* answer to these deep unconscious structures. African film makers such as the Ethiopian Haile Gerima, director of *Harvest: 3,000 Years*,[2] have clearly understood the importance of adopting these structures of perception. They have modelled their narratives on a psychic demand which can perfectly well be satisfied in a completely different manner from the old Indian melodramas which enjoy such great popularity in Africa.[3] Shot very slowly, these old films, whose rhythm is linked to a specific measure of time, have clearly motivated the demands that Tanzanian peasants have made on film makers who want to get them to participate in the production of their own image.[4] But the misguided identification of technological with human progress has often led to the error of colonising the production of a national image through the stereotyped techniques of the modern image industry. This blocks the contribution to culture that could be made by groups which have remained deeply connected with the rhythm of country life, close to the cycle of nature, and still uncontaminated by a system of production which (on the symbolic level at least) is increasingly dominated by sensationalism and ellipsis. At a time when the ideas of development and growth are being called into question by the very countries which do not want to repeat the mistakes of others, is it not also necessary to take account of the contribution these countries can make to the relation between images and filmic time?

The question of women brings us face to face with the same problem. The notion that women, as a dominated group, have of time can be viewed in two ways: on the one hand as alienated, on the other as a positive alternative to the dominant idea of time as geared to linear industrial productivity. There is no doubt that greater value will be attached to the temporality of women as development models are questioned and the limitations of a society governed by the rule of the highest possible GNP becomes plain. Increasingly influential social movements and social theories tell us that work and career are not everything. This new consciousness gives a heightened value to women's work and the patterns of their everyday life. The division of labour which has resulted in the definition of specifically feminine and masculine qualities has reduced the emotional and intellectual capacity of women as much of that of men. And it is now plain that, however urgent it is to increase awareness of the productive value of household tasks, it is also vital to restore value to areas that are not directly productive.

When, in *Jeanne Dielman*, the Belgian director Chantal Ackerman films the everyday banalities of a woman's existence at full length, she does two things at once: she attempts to endow with its own language her subjective experience as a woman, silenced by culture up to now, and at the same time she gives us a creative shock which makes it possible to understand (by contrast) what the customary norm of film time is.

This feminine time is, along with increased awareness of the body, at the heart of the effort being made by women today to give cultural expression to what they as women feel. Beyond the supposedly equal status they may have acquired in the world of production, women are trying to get across what makes them unique and different on the level of subjective experience and symbolic representation. This is leading them to delve into their age-old memory linked to the space and time of reproduction, and in which today part of their specific sensitivity is still shaped. And this is a specific, and unalterably different, sensitivity because it is linked with psychological, biological and sexual differences which have traditionally been used to subordinate them, but which today need to be expressed as an alternative world of symbols and meaning.

It is stimulating to observe that this research seems to be paralleled by the exploration of the time-sense of dominated and marginal races and continents being carried out in, for example, Latin American narrative fiction. This allows us to think that it will really be possible to give a non-alienated answer to the female internalising of the twofold dimension of time – repetition and eternity. Novels such as Gabriel Garcia Marquez's *One Hundred Years of Solitude*, or José Donoso's *The Dark Bird of Night*, are vast epics based on cyclic progress and monumental stretches of time, majestic replies to unconscious demands which provide democratic and liberating outlets, rather than the feeble and imitative products that merely conform to the commercial precepts of market democracy.

3: Information versus fiction

Various studies have clearly brought out the division that can exist within one television channel between *informative* and *fictional* programmes (drama serials, series, etc.), both intended for women, but conveying a different image. One interesting study in this area is *"The influence of audio-visual media on the social and cultural behaviour of women in Japan"*.[1]

The author, Yoko Nuita, shows how, immediately after the end of World War II, the Japanese state broadcasting authority (NHK) helped women to free themselves from their virtual confinement within the family; this was achieved through the programme *Woman's Hour* and even more by group listening to radio, especially to educational programmes. These programmes were entirely in accord with the policy of modernisation in Japan started by the occupying forces, and taking the form, for women, of a policy of emancipation. *Woman's Hour* was then reinforced by another series – *NHK Female Classes* – which dealt with a variety of themes, from problems of family consumption to political, economic and social questions, first on radio, then on television. Around these broadcasts – and this initiative is emblematic of the break that had been made with traditional conceptions of women in media – were set up women's study groups to fight the tendency towards isolation and domestic imprisonment which could have been perpetuated, or even made worse, by solitary listening to broadcasts. Thus, the whole enterprise of civic education for women was served by these NHK programmes, which came to a halt in 1969, partly because Japan's rapid economic development between 1965 and 1969 meant that more and more women took outside jobs, making it difficult to organise daytime group meetings.

It is interesting to note that, by starting to bring women together, the media had in a way played a rôle analogous to work, until economic expansion brought paid work back onto the agenda. Nowadays, there are a certain number of strictly educational programmes which still serve as a focus for female study groups. But we have to interpret this use of the media to promote the development of society in the light of the overall characteristics of media programming in Japan, and particularly of the dominant image of woman transmitted by the media. Nuita says that both drama serials and television plays purvey a stereotyped image of woman. These occupy an enormous amount of programme time, so that traditional social norms are reinforced. "Traditionally the Japanese woman has been brought up to fulfil her rôle as daughter, wife, and mother"; hence, the characters of the "tender mother" or the "good little wife" are dominant. There are a few television plays that show pioneering or resistant female characters, but as a rule "these plays present woman as always willing to conform to the dominant attitude, and go to reinforce traditional female ways of thinking".

This duality can also be observed in some western magazines, especially those which are reluctant to adopt a squarely modernist approach and would rather remain within the confines of a part-traditional, part-modern attitude.[2] The editorials may evince some kind of "progressive" intention, conforming to a mildly liberal image of women in their treatment of permissive morality. But in the same issue, the fiction (a novel serialised over several editions) will portray women in the most conventional light imaginable: passive, dependent, prone to a sugary-sweet view of life.

This leads us to broaden our analysis to take in the media as they generally operate in liberal democracies. Their political function is to reproduce the co-existence of different social classes and groups. Thus, they constitute a place where social tensions are reduced; everybody has a part to play. But at the same time society has to re-assert its cohesiveness by reproducing the legitimacy of public opinion (defined as that of an "average citizen").[3] This "average citizen" – in fact an abstract entity in the service of social inertia –

becomes the basic norm to mediate change and ensure the continuance of tradition. It is in the interests of this basic norm that the balance between information and fiction is established.

This is what the author of the Japanese study says in her remarks on dramatic and other kinds of fiction: "Overall, society demands that women correspond to the rôle of the good wife and good mother. This is why the main characteristic of the female characters in family plays is not a sense of independence, but conformity with existing social standards." Information programmes, on the other hand, meet the demands of other groups, which the media are under an obligation to satisfy if they are to fulfil their task of communication and satisfy divergent interests while mediating their contradictions.

But there is more than one element to take into account. To the crucial question, "What is the relationship between information and fiction?", we have offered two kinds of answer, that given by the Japanese broadcasting system and that given by certain magazines. We could find similar examples in other developing and developed countries. As the territory on which social negotiation takes place, the media make possible – indeed necessary – the co-existence of many varied points of view. The diversity of genres within television and radio, like that of sections within a magazine, expresses (in however trite a way) this necessity, which relates to a rather more complex aspect of the media's answer to the problem of "diversity". We should here point out a fundamental difference which stems from the different places the media occupy in the social structure. Some are under a statutory obligation to favour variety and diversity, others to go further and respect *pluralism*. This distinction is an important one, for it determines the different kinds of answers different media give to a single problem, and thus highlights their specific institutional functions.

A magazine, especially a women's magazine, addresses a fairly consistent and defined public. The magazines that interest us here – those which circulate in accordance with market laws (i.e., not produced by government organisations or political groups) – are usually controlled by a publishing group, answerable only to itself and its public. Its task is to take its public through the different stages of a development whose success is gauged by the volume of sales. Within a group which aims at the female market, a division of labour generally occurs: some magazines cater for the demand of one sector of the population, others for a different kind, and the same holds good for the daily press. So the same group, as we have already seen, will publish photo-novel magazines and modern, not to say *avant-garde*, ones – a distinction known as "down-market" *versus* "up-market" – and both turning out equally professional products. This division of labour, we have suggested, can also arise within one particular magazine, bringing into play a complex but logical array of elements governed by commercial as much as ideological factors. The ideology professed by a magazine is invariably the result of its market positioning (except in a period of crisis; see Part Three).

On the other hand, a medium such as television, especially when it is controlled by criteria of public service, has to give air-time to identifiable public groups whose opinions and ideologies are different, or even incompatible – the very groups that mark the pluralism of a liberal society. The definition of a public service enjoins upon it, in different ways depending on the situation, a rôle of information and social leadership, and of development of democratic life. It has to favour the development of citizens' abilities so that they can be better aware of their rights and better placed to defend them. It also has to show all the major currents of opinion and act as the platform on which society can express itself. *But* it cannot turn itself into an *avant-garde* medium. Its task of ensuring the maintenance of the social order implies a rigorous codification of its pluralism, so that it can cultivate a certain conservatism in the service of the *status quo*. The natural interplay between the informative broadcasts which boost women's rôle and image and the bulk of the fictional ones thus appears as a basic mechanism of this conservatism. The limits of pluralism have been judiciously assessed by Henri Lefèbvre:

"Pluralism admits several ideologies, opinions and moralities. From this liberality it derives a system, banishing dogmatism and opposing repressive systematisation. Quite right too. Yet liberal pluralism itself is systematic and dogmatic in its own way. The number of accepted opinions is few; the liberal accepts several moral codes, but demands some kind of morality. He accepts several religions, but demands some kind of religious sentiment. Old or new, liberalism tends to institutionalize accepted opinions, acceptable moralities or ideologies.... This leads to a tendency to hallow establishment opinions and values."[4]

An essay by a Quebec political scientist, Anne Légaré,[5] about the Canadian national television programme *Today's Woman*, helps us to define what "pluralism" means and the limits it imposes, on itself and others, on the treatment of the female question in liberal society. She stresses that this programme is what it is because of the enterprise of its producer and the intelligence and combativity of her and her team through the past fifteen years (the producer since 1966 has been Michelle Lasnier). At the same time, she points out the inescapable link between this programme and the part played by Radio Canada in the evolution of Canadian society, "a part connected with the support it gives to the multiplicity of groups concerned with social development". The programme's chances of helping social development are connected with the criteria that govern a public service, at one time characterised as the "radical remodelling of all our social, economic and political structures". It was only through tenacious efforts that *Today's Woman* won its nowadays indispensable place on the screen. Through its different phases, this programme contributed decisively, first to helping women fulfil more satisfactorily their rôles as housewives and mothers, through giving credit to their knowledge and articulacy, giving them the necessary tools better to carry out their task in society, and democratising practical knowledge and competence.

Later it helped women to realise who they were, where they were and how changes were affecting them, by describing the development in women's situation (in a couple, in a family or in childhood), by keeping them abreast of social change in Quebec, and by informing them of artistic and literary developments. The fact that the programme nowadays deals less and less with fashion and cooking and more and more with sociology, psychology and education indicates how it has evolved and helped to open out new areas and ideas stemming from the women's movement.

Légaré goes on to show that the image of women constructed in this programme is distinct from that presented by the other programmes on the same channel – whose serials, comedies and advertisements combine to reaffirm the natural dominance of the male. As the producer of the programme herself admits, *Today's Woman* is the programme that best corresponds to the essentials of a public service – "and not by broadcasting songs, either".

But the history of the programme also enables us to catch some element of the *status quo* at work. In the conflicts between the programme's team and audience and the management of the channel, we can (albeit very succinctly) detect the limits of pluralism. *Today's Woman* is currently affected by a crisis of growth, due as much to its fifteen-year-long success as to the specific manner in which its production team conceives female themes. This crisis should be resolved by expansion, or even a multiplication of programmes to cater for the multiplicity of popular demand and the different aspects from which female themes can be viewed. But this lays bare the limits imposed upon "women's programmes" as normally understood in the media, even though these limits can be very markedly extended if the programmes are not conventionally understood by the team in charge of them.[6] It is significant that, when demands were made for this programme to be broadcast at a peak hour, for the benefit of the general public as well as of working women, they were given the thumbs down.

The reason for this refusal – needless to say, never acknowledged openly – was surely that a programme called *Today's Woman* cannot depart from its allocated afternoon slot without calling into question the very standards that govern the channel's programming. If diversity and pluralism require the co-existence of several types of programme, each type is distinguished from the other among other things by the time at which it is broadcast, which corresponds to the conventional division of time in accordance with sex rôles. To adapt Henri Lefèbvre's statement, could we not say that liberal media accept several different ways of conceiving women's rôle and image, but demand some kind of feminine specificity?

One important question still remains. Of the two areas, information and fiction, which has the greater public impact, from the nebulous point of view of its "effects" – i.e., the attitudes, ambitions and models it transmits? To answer this, we really need an extensive study of audiences, in an interdisciplinary perspective, combining the approaches of sociology, anthropology, psychoanalysis and semiology. This may be highly controversial. We should begin by pointing out that it has long been recognised by cultural critics that mass culture brings together a variety of different areas: the "real" and the "imaginary" [in their Lacanian sense – trans.], the effect of fictional conventions upon the field of information, the sensationalist tendency of that field and so forth. The boundary between reality and fiction becomes progressively more vague. In this sense, *Today's Woman* seems to be an exception to the rule: for us it clearly belongs in the field of information, even though its channel is an "entertainment" one – yet further confirmation of the ideology implicit in the definition of a woman's programme! The effect of fictional standards upon the field of information, conversely, can be seen in most women's radio or television broadcasts.

Rather than trying to give a hard and fast answer to the question, we shall simply identify where the conflict is, drawing attention to the importance of fiction for reasons other than the amount of air-time it takes up. We are inclined on balance to think that fiction has a greater impact upon the majority of people than informative programmes. A lifestyle is more easily transmitted fictionally than non-fictionally. Fictional programmes – serials, series, family comedies – are the places where the feelings and ideas of the "silent majority" are confirmed, where accepted wisdom on the hierarchy of rôles and values is reiterated and rearranged in such a way as to reinforce the beliefs and practices of the greatest number. They are also the place where disruptive elements are digested, and non-conformist ideas absorbed. This zone of mass culture is the privileged space where authority does not need to speak politically in order to act politically.

Fiction and information do not refer to the same things. However influenced by fictional values they may be, information programmes still refer to *reality*. Fictional programmes refer to another text, the already-said, the already-written. Reality manifests tension, effort, history, and an openness to the future, the developing, the unknown. The already-said reiterates the past and renews the sense of security which it is its main business to provide.

Part Two

Modernity

1: The feminine ideal

The process of internationalisation is so often approached on a global scale that it is easy to forget that transnational firms have a country of origin. The successful models, the touchstones for the cultural mass production of advanced capitalism, come from the American multimedia conglomerates. On close examination, it becomes clear that very few other developed countries have created systems that can be standardised and reproduced on a world scale.[1] For example, French television dramas are rarely exported outside France's exclusive markets (mainly former colonies) and rarely become models for producing a marketable culture; and this is only one symptom of a situation which is undoubtedly dominated by the North American leisure industry.

National stereotypes, which reflect the domestic economic context and the particular nature of the contradictions in a given society, always betray their origin. For our purposes, and in the case of France, sufficient evidence of this is provided by the magazines *Elle* and *Marie-Claire*, which cannot be judged in the same category as American magazines. On the other hand, a magazine such as *Cosmopolitan*,[2] which is now produced in local versions both in Europe and Latin America, is based on an American model, and contains a variable proportion of the U.S. edition. Another example of a different kind of derivation is *F Magazine* (launched in France in 1978), and inspired by *Ms*, a liberal feminist magazine in the United States.[3] Isn't it the case, therefore, that as a country increasingly applies the development model based on the expansion of transnational capital, it feels obliged to resort to the formulae which have proved to be most effective in this context?

For these reasons and for many others, it may be useful to explore the origins of this particular model with pretensions of universality, and to note some of the stages in the formation of the "feminine ideal". To do this it is necessary to go back to the launching of this ideal by the cultural industries (advertising, in particular) in the 1920s in the United States.

At that time the women's suffrage movement had created a particular political climate, and industrialisation seemed to promise women an escape from their confinement in the home. At this point also, there emerged what we have described as the ideology of *modernity*, which helped both to disseminate a notion of change and to orientate the development of women in a direction compatible with the performance of their established social rôle as wife and mother.

With the publication of her book *Selling Mrs Consumer* in 1929, Christine Frederick became the standard-bearer for the new consumer ideology. She defined this as follows:

"Consumptionism is the name given to the new doctrine; and it is admitted today to be the greatest idea that America has to give to the world – the idea that workmen and masses be looked upon not simply as workers and producers, but as *consumers* ... Pay them more, sell them more, prosper more is the equation."[4]

The implication of this was that the household was beginning to live at the pace of the industrial world, and that the home was becoming a market.

The new feminine ideal was thus presented in the form of the modern housewife who "is no longer a cook – she is a can-opener" (in the words of C. Frederick). The household was urged to open its doors to industrial products and to stop being a closed domain where the reproduction of life was ensured through traditional feminine activities and the traditional practices of mending, hand sewing, laundering, home cooking, simmering, reheating, etc. The awakening of industry's interest in the home required that the housewife should learn to get accustomed to the principles of the market.

Her rôle in the household was upgraded and at the same time modified in the direction imposed by the new criteria of rationalisation and technology. Hence, traditional and "homecraft" knowledge was regarded with condescension as a set of old wives' tales born of superstition. The approaches adopted in advertising campaigns, first in magazines, then on radio and television, glorified this new concept: the traditional image of the woman as a "domestic slave" was shattered.[5] As the result of new discoveries applied by industry, the housewife's rôle became exciting and fulfilling. Routine work was giving way to creativity.[6] Technology was enhancing the old order of things by virtue of its sophistication. The household, open to all the new promises of comfort, wellbeing and interior decoration, was depicted as a place where the housewife could give free rein to her talents, develop her imagination, and use all the skills she would have otherwise used outside the home. Advertising and women's magazines constantly played on the attractiveness of this fulfilment in a household open to the ever-changing outside market. The situation has not altered since. Advertising approaches, constantly updated, still try to make women feel she has a power of control and a *savoir-faire* that is circumscribed only by the ideology of the market. She is "a good shopper".

In this strategy of recycling, the rôle of the mother is given new importance as well. In 1922, *Ladies' Home Journal* already featured many articles on child rearing and gave advice on useful books to read. In doing so, it was responding to the mother's feelings of anxiety and insecurity, and at the same time cultivating them. Here, once again, the tendency was to strip mothers of their intuitive knowledge, and to place them under the power of the new scientific knowledge. Baby food advertisements eagerly adopted this new tone of scientific authority, and described in glowing terms how their product satisfied the requirements of hygiene, balanced nutrition, etc., thus commercially cultivating the mother's guilty feelings.

This new image, which linked the expanding consumer goods market with the political climate created by the women's vote, and which modernised the traditional rôle of women in order to prevent a search for novelty from finding outlets elsewhere, thus perpetuated discrimination in terms of rôles and spheres of action. The ideological world of the man was the world of production; the world of the woman was consumption. In the new industrial age, the cultural world of women did indeed break free from traditional forms of patriarchal authority; but at the same time it fell into the hands of a new authority in the form of the industrial rationale of companies, and the scientific know-how of specialists.[7]

When Betty Friedan published *The Feminine Mystique* in 1963, the new feminine ideal seemed to be more firmly established than ever. Even the Second World War, in which women were recruited into the labour force, had not altered this ideal. On the contrary, immediately after the war, as a result of the feelings of desolation and loneliness it had cultivated, the feminine mystique came into its full glory, reaching a climax in 1959. Over-simplifications of Freudian theories, and misinterpretations of Margaret Mead's anthropological studies of sexual rôles in the primitive populations of the South Seas, were called in to rescue the feminine ideal. Aggressiveness in women was described, for example, as a mere manifestation of their "castration complex". Supported by the commercial forces at work behind the idea of a "feminine mystique", the ideological system which regards the home as the woman's "natural" place found overwhelming acceptance during this period.

The impact of this model of femininity is confirmed by the picture given by Betty Friedan of the development of women's participation in productive, salaried work. Despite the rapid economic expansion in the United States between 1900 and 1950, and the accelerated pace of urbanisation, the proportion of women in employment rose by a mere 8.1 per cent (from 20.4 to 28.5 per cent) over this period. Although the proportion of women in higher education rose from 21 to 47 per cent between 1870 and 1920, it had dropped to only 35.2 per cent by 1958. In the 1950s, there were five times more women in the medical profession in France than in the United States. At the same time, 70 per cent of all Soviet doctors were women, while in the United States the proportion was only 5 per cent.[8] In the 1950s, women wage-earners were mostly young women in the eighteen to nineteen-year bracket, or married women or widows over forty-five. Most of them had jobs requiring no special qualifications. Only one third worked full time; another third worked full time only at certain times of the year (i.e., salesgirls hired for peak sales periods such as Christmas); and the last third worked part time only for part of the year. The overwhelming majority of professional women were single. Married women over forty-five in employment were (like the eighteen to nineteen-year-olds) bunched at the bottom of the scales of wages and qualifications.[9]

The ideology of the housewife had paid off and demonstrated its usefulness to capital. If women consider themselves primarily as wives and mothers, and only secondarily as workers, they are much less likely to demand an interesting job and a wage which gives them economic independence. Women who have internalised the secondary value of their work outside the home are easily induced to serve as cheap labour, recruited at peak periods and hired and fired according to the ups and downs of the economy.

Today, the participation of women in employment and the range of jobs held by women have both changed considerably. The woman who prepares herself for a career and the career woman are no longer rarities. One striking feature is the close similarity between the picture of women's employment during the 1950s and 1960s in a society in full expansion, and the present structure of women's employment, which television series and family serials claim to reflect. We shall refer here to a study which analyses a large number of serials broadcast in North America, Belgium and France during the years 1973–75.[10] These serials show several trends, one being towards a solidity with "documentary" pretensions, another more abstract and closer to the espionage genre; but all were designed for family audiences.

These serials do give value to women's work; but even so it is never something desirable *per se*. The work of a woman is always regarded as a substitute for a husband (the one she doesn't have, or doesn't yet have, or has lost), or for the love she longs to receive or that she seeks to give. Women's work is regarded as legitimate only as a form of compensation. It is a secondary territory (the *first and foremost* being the home) for the conventional signs of femininity to be manifested. Women's dependence on their family rôle is depicted as the very essence of womanhood: their fulfilment can be achieved only in conformity with their husband's wishes. The difference between the old model and the new is resolved: unlike the traditional family model, the present-day model does not require the husband to express a wish which must be obeyed. The wishes of the husband are now perceived by the wife to be her own wishes. Thus, subordination is experienced as freedom. A woman's primary rôle is imposed on her by the predominance of her duties as wife and mother. Any other rôle appears secondary and superfluous, if not detrimental to the proper performance of her first rôle.

This similarity between the sociological picture of earlier times and the manner in which the subject is treated in the present-day context of television serials is highly significant. It would seem to indicate a certain permanence in the cultural definition of women, despite the fact that the reality of their lives has changed. And it is precisely in this failure of the media to keep up with current sociological reality, and with the actual world of today in which women have more opportunities to work, that we can discern most clearly the regulatory rôle of mass culture, which gives new life to an out-dated vision of reality in order to hold in check any possible excesses of the present, and their subversive influence.

Contemporary women's magazines also support, both implicitly and explicitly, this dichotomy between primary and secondary occupations and primary and secondary rôles; and they tend to establish an equivalence between women's work and maternity. As noted by Anne-Marie Dardigna, who has studied French women's magazines, this is true of magazines as different as *Bonne Soirée*, *Vogue*, *Elle* and *Marie-Claire*.[11] Women's work outside the home is deemed to be incompatible with her other work as a mother. Attention is drawn to the conflicts resulting from the *double working day* of the working mother. This is described in women's magazines in depressing terms: "Problems are often insurmountable. The list is familiar: overwork, nervousness, failure to meet the children as they come out of school, the difficulties of treating them when they are ill, the difficulty of selecting holiday dates which coincide, etc."[12] As a solution to these problems, the magazine does not suggest a fairer division of household tasks and childcare between husband and wife, or a possible socialisation of household chores, but resorts instead to a mystification of the problem: maternity becomes a career. The practical details and repercussions of such an assertion (What is the salary? What are the hours? Which trade union?) are entirely ignored. This mystification is consistent with the reader's own understanding of her "natural rôle". Apart from magazines such as *Cosmopolitan* and, of course, magazines which are organs of liberal feminist groups (such as *Ms* in the United States and *F Magazine* in France) women's magazines as a whole promote the dominant idea of the housewife.

Working women

At the end of the 1960s, the "working woman" became a new target for magazine publishers and advertising agents. In their professional journals, advertising men gave their reasons for believing in this new market: "By 1980, an estimated 46% of all women will be bringing home a pay check. Will the working woman market run right past you?" ... "As an advertiser, it'll pay to find out how this growth will affect you." ... "Reaching today's working wife may prove to be the most challenging, rewarding, and lucrative job you'll ever have. How to woo the working woman."[13] In France, the arrival of *Cosmopolitan* and the creation of *F Magazine* coincided with the emergence of a new image of women which was to lead to changes in the editorial content and promotional strategies of the older magazines. The aim was to develop a narcissistic dimension, as opposed to the earlier family dimension, the incentive to buy.

We do not intend to dwell on this last point, but would like to examine the split which occurred on the last issue of sexual morality between the older magazines and the new. Let us briefly compare *Good Housekeeping* and *Cosmopolitan*, two American magazines both published by the Hearst group. *Cosmopolitan* is not a new title in the United States but the phenomenon of transnationalisation has transformed it, in recipient countries, into a magazine which breaks with the traditional model of the mother in the home. On the other hand, the liberation of the housewife presented by *Good Housekeeping* never takes her too far from her kitchen; and sexuality is still confined to the context of marriage and the family. This model of sexuality orientated towards reproduction within the family – a model which the magazine continues to promote – is an accurate reflection of the model still prevalent in real life. *Cosmopolitan*, on the other hand, purports to be a magazine primarily concerned with feminine sexuality. The women featured in this magazine are economically independent and, above all, sexually aggressive and sensual: the magazine publishes articles on socio-psychological problems and conflicts related to sexuality – a sexuality no longer defined in the context of reproduction, although marriage to one partner chosen from among the many partners is seen as an ultimate goal.

This representation of feminine sexuality undeniably opens up a new and original potential, since sexuality is no longer governed by the rules of a repressive code; but its potential is channelled into a marketing process accentuated by the imagery of the all-too-prevalent advertisements. *Cosmopolitan* indulges, for instance, in commercialisation of parts of the body not previously defined as sexual (eyes, lips, ears, skin, teeth) and the sexualisation of situations and places in which sexuality was previously taboo (employment and the street). However, this leads to contradictions in the magazine's position: on the one hand, advertisers exploit the subversive potential of the new depiction of feminine sexuality; on the other, the highly narcissistic self-discovery which the magazine encourages women to undertake parallels "the explicit politicization of sexuality by the women's movement – a politicization to effect transformations in the social position of women".[14]

There is a similar split between the two French magazines *Bonne Soirée* and *Elle*. From the late 1960s onwards, *Elle* played an important rôle in the legalisation of abortion, and championed the claims of women who wished to be able to freely control their bodies and plan their maternities. Readers of *Bonne Soirée*, on the other hand, were presented with a highly repressive moral code which in 1980 was still condemning abortion and giving extensive coverage to the Church's position on the subject.

Commercial magazines which support the liberal feminist movement may, when viewed from another angle, reveal similar contradictions. Leftist critics have accused them with some justification (at least in the case of *F Magazine*) of tending to present the new feminine normality in terms only of changes that have occurred in the lives of upper-class women who have had the necessary higher education and training to enter a profession on an "equal footing", so to speak, with men of their own milieu.[15] Although these critics cannot deny that the magazines in question are transmitting a more encouraging and stimulating image of women, they deplore the fact that the same magazines are also accomplices in the involvement of the women's liberation movement in the commercial market. They complain that the magazines do not show any real solidarity with working-class women, their struggles, sit-in strikes, etc., but display their feminist bias in a manner consistent with the norms of competition advocated by the system. In short, they never tackle the question of *sexist ideology as the basis of the capitalist system.*

It remains to be seen whether or not this judgement is too hasty, and whether it neglects to take into account the way in which these magazines deal with questions relating to the organisation of society – questions that women of the liberal movements, with their new awareness, are bound to raise. Only a close examination of these magazines will enable us to answer these questions. In its January 1981 issue, *Ms* Magazine published a special report denouncing conditions of work for women workers in the electronics industry on the border between the United States and Mexico, and in South-East Asia. This extensive investigation showed that the new international division of labour, in which the production process is split up into parts (the parts being dispersed all over the world, though the control of the entire process and of the technology remains in the hands of central managements in the controlling countries, the United States and Japan in particular) relies essentially on the exploitation of women workers from third world countries.[16]

These women have become a key resource for the expansion of transnational capital. Unskilled women workers in the Spanish-American countries and South-East Asia account for nearly ninety per cent of the assembly workers in transnational electronics firms. Underpaid, these women perform extremely monotonous, boring, repetitive and dangerous tasks. The work of assembling micro-components requires intense visual concentration and constant finger movement, which frequently leads to nervous breakdowns and cerebral damage. This exploitation of women is based on a traditional view of women as placid, patient, submissive, meticulous, uncomplaining, respectful of authority, clever with their hands, and slow to organise themselves. Their low wages are said to be due to their lack of professional skills, but are in fact based on codes of sexual repression which are still prevalent in highly patriarchal societies which impose severe economic, political and social sanctions on work by women, because it transgresses certain taboos. These methods of organisation and authoritarian control are fully in keeping with the expansionist requirements of the transnational firms, these major units of modern capital, which are confronted in their home countries with progressive labour laws, trade unions and critical currents of opinion. In developing countries, they even give the impression of being outposts of modernity, since the working conditions they offer are slightly better than those in local enterprises.

This investigation did not confine itself to denouncing the sexist implications of the exploitation of the labour force in third world countries. It also showed these practices at work in the United States where, with cut-throat competition in light industry, small firms, in defiance of the law and other controls, exploit the illicit labour of women workers (most of them Chinese and Puerto Rican) who, despite their vulnerability, are beginning to form unions.

This demonstrates how a magazine can echo the content of campaigns now being undertaken by many women to prove that the passive/active woman dichotomy is in some ways false, and explain how the sexist ideology underlying the so-called "passivity" of women and their confinement to the home (considered as their primary domain of activity) also rules their status at work and predisposes them to be the first victims of the new – as of the old – division of labour.[17]

2: The myth of modernity

"An article that will keep you up to date on today's make-up and make you laugh about what they said yesterday. Plus the photos of the decade."
Vanidades Continental

The concept of modernity has assumed the rôle of a banner, a watchword in the production of goods and symbols in capitalist industrial society. A thorough inquiry into this concept may therefore prove one of the more worthwhile ways of approaching the guiding principle of a system of social control which justifies its dynamism and its notion of progress by repeating *ad nauseam* the litany of constant improvement and technological happiness through unlimited consumption. Among the words describing the benefits and achievements of this ruling society, unifying and glorifying them, and thus contributing to their fertile reproduction, there is a key term: modernity. Among its peers and synonyms can be found: fashion, today's world, new, and novel, always with a disdainful glance towards yesterday; and paradoxically so, since we will have more than one occasion to catch them in worship at the shrine of "tradition".

Marx showed that when the bourgeoisie rose to power, they delayed the process of history and froze the notion of movement. The bourgeois regime interprets capitalist order not as a transitory phase of the historical process, but rather as the absolute form of social production. This same holding back of history obliges them ceaselessly to renew their reserve of arguments designed to make the dominated believe that the solutions that they propose for human liberation and happiness are the definitive ideal of civilization and culture. Having established their order in this rigid form, having naturalised and eternalised it, one of the most sensitive areas of bourgeois mystification becomes that involving the concept of change. By disguising the origin of this concept, they try to cover up the fact that, in the final analysis, the notion of change which the bourgeoisie promotes amounts to nothing more than its repudiation.

After a hegemony in distinguished grey, presided over by the figures of the judge and the legislator, guardians of bourgeois legal political ideology, and where, in the privacy of the home, the stock market prices were faithfully consulted in the liberal morning press, there now explodes an irreverent splash of colour and extravagance, the advertising bazaar of technological society. And the passage from this earlier order to apparent anarchy brought with it a new-style bourgeoisie, a new kind of imperialism, a new kind of social regulation, operating essentially through the mass communications apparatus. The concepts which once cemented bourgeois institutions and ensured a consensus on the profile of the perfect citizen – law-abiding and respectful of representative democracy and established morals – seem to be overridden by science and technology. These now take part in a daily routine which craves happiness and which evinces no kinship with the harsh mechanics of the dawn of industrialisation nor, to use another image, with the stuffy formality of the parliaments. In other words, a technocratic ideology has superseded the formerly dominant legal political sphere. But this time, domination (hidden, disguised) is exercised through extremely diversified channels, allowing a much more total infiltration of everyday life. Its powers are multiplied, and now attempt to satisfy every possible need. The noticeable shift in the ideological centre of gravity from the legal political sphere to the technocratic sphere signifies a shift in the nucleus of the symbols which are articulated in the power strategy. This substitution is obviously adapted to a particular moment in the development of the productive forces, since it protects, in a more functional way, the interests of the hegemonic centre.

We shall here try to analyse how modernity has become an ideology of constant movement and progression, daily regeneration and effervescent mutation, masking the static quality of the structures which generated it. Our objective is to look at the insistent modernity imposed upon us every day by society – advertising jingles, elegant fashions, new styles, artificial atmospheres, plasticity, cleverness – as well as the ensemble of images, the spiritual and motivating dimensions which ensure an individual and collective response. In other words, we will try to bring to light certain aspects of the myths which have been devised to create or, more precisely, replenish cultures so they can work within the modernising concept of social development. Within the pattern of dependency, we must point out (even when it seems obvious) that this replenishment of the superstructure aggravates its disparity with the infrastructure. The awakened desires, the patterns of behaviour, the euphoria of consumption proposed by the ideology of modernity and radiated by the imperialist core countries, are increasingly removed from anything really possible, given the structures of production and the purchasing power of most sections of society. The ideology of modernity is an integral part of a superstructure which conceives of revolution as genetically technological and, in its principle lines, antithetic to socialist revolution. Deciphering this ideology requires a close examination of new forms of control over behaviour and aspirations, and a reading of the symbols which express its existence in everyday life.

A first approach to the myth

As a starting point from which substantially to challenge the concept of modernity we have chosen to examine magazines directed at women, knowing full well that among the many obstacles they present to the researcher are undoubtedly their apparent triviality or insignificance, as well as their restriction to very specific interests. Without trying to be pompous, we could suggest that the treatment of the topic of women's magazines already has antecedents in the sociological, semiological and philosophical studies of people as well known as Edgar Morin, Roland Barthes and Henri Lefèbvre – all French by some strange coincidence – and also, perhaps with a different intention and focus, the work of Adorno and Horkheimer, who studied the whole area of cultural industry. Our choice of the topic of women's magazines has, however, more substantial reasons: for while apparently specific, this subject has increasingly broadened out. The press in general, as well as the ensemble of the mass media (film, radio or television) are continually being colonised by these feminine-style values which together make up a stereotype of femininity: values ruled by the heart, domestic activity, everyday life and intimacy are obsessively present in all the products of the cultural industry.

It is easy to demonstrate the gravitation of these ideas and values towards advertising. The entire thrust of the so-called revolution of rising expectations finally converges in women. Furthermore (and here we are struck by the compact totality of the phenomenon), electoral propaganda has adopted as an unspoken central idea the theme of the mother and child – calling to mind femininity, childhood, innocence and helplessness. The right uses these images quite openly to determine and prescribe a kind of behaviour aimed at preserving the liberal order and repelling any attempt to alter it, in a violent or non-violent way. "Political" marketing techniques simply take advantage of the symbols used by commercial advertising. Now, we can clearly perceive the "universal" value of the images, manipulated by the dominant ideology, when, in the same electoral contests, the Left, for tactical reasons (and often, lack of strategy) uses these same themes of the woman and child. This leads to a crystallisation of defensive attitudes, centred primarily in the sphere of private interests and the security of the family. The family is the last stage, the most subtle and yet the most certain, in the social reproduction of the state apparatus, the last stage of "civil society". This is the strength of the stereotype of femininity in our societies, in its traditional or its modernised version. By the mere hidden power of the image, by its simple insinuations, a woman's face – and we are not referring here to the "stars" – calls to mind non-aggression, security, legitimacy and compromise.

Women's magazines

Let us leave for the moment this myth of femininity, which equates the idea of woman with the negation of change or, if you prefer, this mythical antagonism between woman and change, and turn to the concept of modernity, trying to explain how it is processed by the dominant ideology, especially through women's magazines, as an alibi for change: how modernity reaffirms the myth of femininity, giving it a new validity, a new justification.

This antagonism between the concepts woman/change essentially goes back to the fact that, in all cultures, myths associate the image of the woman with the life-giving elements: earth and water, elements of fertility and permanence. The image of woman is linked to the idea of continuity, perpetuation, timelessness. Against the transient nature of upheavals, crises and chaos, corresponding to the concept of change, is played and contrasted the cyclic timing of woman, which traces concentric lines leading forever back to the starting point, unifying past, present and future. This is a time which flows, in which the eternal rôles are performed: marriage, home, motherhood. The pattern of a woman's life is portrayed as the antithetical justification of, and compensation for, the pattern of a man's life, whose action is inscribed in the dialectic of a reality of struggle and domination of the world.

With the development of technology, it became necessary to introduce the notion of modernity, modernity as representation and practice, in order to create a semblance of newness, to say nothing of revolution, in social life, and especially in women's lives. Change, in as much as it affects women, became synonymous with integration into the "modern". And it is the image of the happy woman, the woman dazzled by the desires and possibilities of consumption, the desires and possibilities of progress, which is the best publicity for modernity, fostering the immersion of technology into daily life: woman becomes the "smile of modernity".

Women's magazines cultivate and diffuse this myth of the modern as a universal model – a model founded on a cliché of the woman from a very comfortable socio-economic group in an industrialised capitalist society. Of course this model fantasises considerably on the situation of these women, extrapolating the well-being, freedom and pleasure which they have attained in their daily lives. A very general analysis exposes two levels of alienation: the first, inherent in the model itself, eulogises the life-style, the atmosphere and purchasing power attained by a particular class in a "developed" country; the second more or less mechanically transplants this model to the reality of a dependent country. Relating this to a local context, we might point out that a Chilean magazine such as *Paula*, edited by a group of upper middle class Chilean women, does not manifest the same scandalously dependent character as does *Vanidades Continental*, edited in Miami and distributed throughout Latin America, even though both magazines are published by the same company and under the same trademark.

It is the pattern of social stratification implied in these magazines which furnishes both the departure point for the myth and its reference point. Even if the magazine evokes or describes other life-styles, even if it refers to other social groups, in the final analysis all the heavily promoted articles, all the news, all the centres of interest, the preoccupations, are subordinated to the all-powerful normalising pattern whose perspective deflects any opportunity to establish the message within a socially given reality. The amorphous society proposed is far from innocent, since it revolves around an illusion of the class which has the greatest chances of entering this fantasy world.

The examples are legion.

A "letter to the editor" from a young office worker tells of her anxiety about inviting her section head and fellow workers to her home, which is located in a rather precarious, low-prestige neighbourhood. The reply leaves unanswered the writer's real concern, that she is ashamed of her social position and afraid to reveal it. The solution presented – almost unconsciously – makes use of the supreme artifice, suggesting the use of wallpaper with a novel design along with other decorative tricks, as a way of getting through this hierarchical confrontation unscathed. In other words, to underline this example, all the symbols "to be found at your fingertips" are really the symbols from the universe of a class which distributes them with a paternal gesture and confers upon this aesthetic benefaction the value of an initiation, the revelation of a secret code. It couldn't be otherwise, since the norm which regulates all the articles on interior decorating, for example, is based invariably on houses, gardens and neighbourhoods pertaining to a limited sector of the bourgeoisie. The bohemian fantasy of "doing up" an attic, a forgotten corner of an old mansion, is a far cry from the urgent need to redecorate an office worker's only room.

"A newlywed couple, architecture students, have made their home above a garage. It's small but very cheerful. The trick was in the simplicity of everything they put inside." Although certain items shown in the accompanying photos (an ultra-modern stereo system, geometrical and folding furniture bought from the exclusive distributor) contradict the low-key complacency of the description in the text, in reality the total effect is indeed achieved through colour and simplicity. But these come across as qualities devoid of their present-day significance in the market and stripped of their stylish connotation: after having run the whole semantic gamut to describe the bareness and scarcity, simplicity emerges as the key to this atmosphere of modern exquisiteness, making simplicity an expensive taste.

"Their house, so typically Chilean, cried out to be photographed. It was constructed with the intention of maintaining the Chilean style of open houses, full of patios and corridors, yet cozy – and above all inexpensive, because their budget was limited." The article felt obliged to emphasise that this dream house, offered to the eyes of the readers, could fit into an open, democratic structure, and could correspond to a profile of a prospective buyer (low-cost, easy payments, savings and loans). Again, the text minimises, excuses and tries to remain detached from the visual spectacle – the élitist splendour spreading through colonial corridors, sun patios, private terraces, indescribable bathrooms, and regenerated in every decorative novelty and symbol: a Manila shawl, an antique sideboard, etc. It is from this pinnacle of refinement that the Chilean essence is supposed to radiate. Yet a simple transposition of context strips the myth bare.[1]

The apparent universality of this pattern – as if the lifeblood of the bourgeoisie flowed through the veins of the entire population – vanishes into thin air when this archetype is confronted with the empirical reality into which it is supposed to fit, a reality which is obsessively dialectical and chaotic. By confronting the model with the reality in which it operates, its mythical aspect can clearly be seen. By abstracting a pattern of social stratification, and polarizing it into a class, women's magazines have succeeded in eliminating from their vision the struggle against a mode of production which allows a few to benefit from what the majority have produced.

It seems unnecessary to follow these first observations on the mythical aspect of modernity by emphasising the importance of fashion as a universal determining factor in women's magazines. Fashion as an aspiration and bond for all women, usurping the function of democracy, or using democracy as an alibi, can be seen as an implicit attempt to wipe out any trace of conflict within society, and substitute the ideology of fashion/modernity for the necessity of a critical consciousness. This process is orchestrated by the whole numbing apparatus which provides the euphoria of images and vocabulary that have become a basic element in the system of style.

Supplement: women's liberation

Further on, we shall examine how the image of women being promoted by this type of magazine has adopted certain characteristics which make up the traditional or conformist model. We shall attempt to show that the change which this image undergoes is minimal, never trespassing outside the limits defined by modernity, and never showing any real rebellion against the principles of the system. In other words, as far as the image of the female entity diffused by these magazines is concerned, we can hypothesise that in bourgeois ideology change is subject to the condition of invariability.

And in this sense it is surprising to find this fixation in women's magazines for all those "traditional" topics geared to "heart economics": the letters from the lovelorn, serialised novels, horoscopes; or geared to that other fundamental and obligatory axis, the duties of the housewife: "home economics". For example, a special section, "Supplement: Women's Liberation", accompanying *El Mercurio*, Wednesday, 30 June 1971, was announced as a series of articles specially dedicated to the woman and *her world, the home* (our emphasis). The deliberately deceitful, emancipating title was a trap, a way of disguising and, at the same time, subversively revitalising the contents it represented. Such articles, which testify to the anti-intellectual, obscurantist prejudice of bourgeois ideology concerning women, have as their implicit and ultimate goal the refinement of the isolation of the female being – on the one hand within the inessential and the frivolous, and on the other, within a world apart, cut off from concrete global reality: at home. When a woman's intellectual or artistic value is recognized, this new attribute is made to function very much like that of style: neither existential nor experiential, but rather symbolic, representing status or class. Furthermore, these "extra" functions are always subordinate in bourgeois mythology, which emphasizes the superior, determinant validity of the eternal rôles. The woman who writes novels, and who, as a writer, irradiates the image of an artist, with a dose of the bohemian, must, in order not to be seen as a rebel, prove her submission to the eternal status of femininity.

Having silenced the only concrete frame of reference, that of society, women's magazines have come to base themselves on what is "natural" and on those attributes considered intrinsic to women. Here we perceive the point of fusion between the traditional and the modern; the message which segregates its interests according to the definition of the audience, implicitly defined and accepted as a subordinate group, then renews its links with the elements of tradition in order to promote a new archetype. The argument of woman's nature – the only common denominator in this system – becomes an argument of authority, enclosing the emancipation and liberation of women within the very limits of their gender: "delicately feminine"; "romantically feminine"; "to make you a real woman"; "every design, every outfit, every detail was created delicately, so that this season you will be more feminine, more a woman . . . and in style." Advertising never escapes this tautological circle in which women's liberation is expressed. But the terms feminine-feminising which are used to describe all the new concepts (and in particular those with subversive possibilities) are self-limiting. In a masochistic-euphorial tension, flirtatiousness, the desire to be found attractive, the woman-as-prey, are all given modern authority through women's magazines, and the relations of woman-world and woman-man which are implied therein are revalidated, confirmed and eternalised. "Bring them to their knees", "feel deadly", steal the show"; "be an attention-getter" thanks to exhibitionist boots or imported perfumes, which, while reaching the height of a supposedly emancipating process, in reality keep assimilating women's evolution into the competition and dynamism of fashion. The nucleus of the implicit theory of women's liberation projected by this model consists in rescuing her from the privacy of the home and launching her into an outside world where she can be individualised and liberated thanks to a competition based on the acquisition of goods and the fervent respect for fashion. But our remarks on this phenomenon would not be complete without recalling an image so profusely reiterated in the ads for masculine clothing and cosmetics. The woman graphically assumes a position of a sophisticated slave, thrown at the feet of the man who conquers and dominates her, an attitude which materialises the old balance of rôles, those of the master and the servant. *The traditional is confirmed and eternalized in the modern.*

It can be argued that this model of modernity also favours types of behaviour which do not ordinarily fit into traditional patterns of conduct. Among them, *work*. Even if it does constitute a topic of greater complexity, its emancipating value is still impaired by the unrealistic treatment to which it is submitted. Work is stripped of its experience, and not only work which allows a woman to leave the domestic scene, but work in general. It takes on an exalted appearance; it is the ingredient of a happy world, with no bodily or material resistance. Physical and psychological hazards are overcome. Frustrations, conflicts, the all-powerful hierarchy, all vanish into thin air. "Why do you insist on showing the woman who comes home from the office as if she were someone returning from a party?" It is a disfigurement of the reality. But as the question indicates, not all the readers allow themselves to be taken in by the iconography.

By not taking into account the concrete conditions of life and capacity for work, women's magazines resign themselves to illustrating the notion of work as if it were a miraculous therapy – when, in reality, work is often the foremost instrument of alienation and creator of points of conflict. The airplane mechanic poses, smiling, impeccable, next to the model who sports the same helmet as he does. By resorting to symbols of the work sphere (commonly connoted by participation in advanced technology – or almost the opposite, as we shall see later on, by its fusion with nature), the fashion show is allowed a superficial, fictitious contact with the concrete world and the reality of everyday life which, through a movement of interaction, also becomes a show, the decor of leisure. Or else, they try to plant fashion in a "popular setting": we increasingly see photographs of fashion collections set in the most primitive villages, those farthest away from technical civilisation.

Two parallel orders

A comparison between two types of women's publications – women's magazines on the one hand, and "romance" magazines on the other – will illustrate the fact that modernity is morphology, restoring a permanent, identical content and a norm whose aim is to promote conformism. Between "romance" and "women's" magazines, the first and foremost distinction is in the area of visual perception. It exists on the level of morphology. And relying on an earlier study of "romance" publications,[2] it's clear that their contents are guided by the same principles and achieve their coherence in an identical semantic structure, significant of an overall purpose: that of maintaining a particular order. Or, if we reject the disassociation of form and content, and come face to face with the message as a specific technology whose content and form interact and mutually determine one another, we can say that both examples are functional to the system; that the rhetoric which unfolds in both of them is functional to the extent that both are based on escapism, the romance magazines in the "traditional" sense, the women's magazines in the "modern", and that they both absolve the existing structures.

It is also important to go beyond this purely visual differentiation between the two types of publications directed at women. On closer examination, the themes which they embrace, the orders which they encode, actually translate the different ideological zones in which they operate: the area of the heart, on the one hand, and the area of consumption on the other, each one accompanied by particular ways of promoting a certain kind of behaviour in their readers.

Both products of modern capitalism, "women's" (fashion, etc.) magazines and "romance" magazines (*fotonovelas*) pertain nonetheless to particular moments and different mechanisms of bourgeois domination. They are complementary. Of course, the "romance" magazines have a greater tendency to develop under the obscurantism promoted by fascism and other present-day authoritarian regimes, where their circulation surpasses that of the "modern" magazines. Yet they are equally present within the normal framework of liberal democracy. The "women's" magazines, on the other hand, correspond to the "enlightened" dimension of the ruling class. The two genres express the different alliances which the bourgeoisie seeks to establish with women from the various layers of society. And the variations which can be found, according to the historical moment, in the predominance of one genre over the other, are inseparably related to the type of consensus which the bourgeois state can induce (and the model of development which it patronises).[3]

The layout of women's magazines is defined by the demands and criteria of modernity, which can be characterised in terms of slickness, ingeniousness, variety, avant-garde photography and, in a word, luxury. The relative scarcity of these examples of modernity in the romance magazines, which are guided more by triviality and banality, is just another indication of the segregation which prevails in "mass" communications media, and particularly within those intended for specific audiences. In reality, the media are impregnated with an idea of culture, a structure of taste which reflects a discriminatory pattern: luxury, refinement, vanguardist design, for some; persistence of obsolete forms, gloomy iconography, poor quality design for others. The deceptively *universalising* modernity of taste and culture, despite its rhetoric of standardisation, nevertheless must ultimately respect the scales imposed by empirical reality, the reality of class society, even if it is only to continue the task which falls to it in the division of labour under monopolistic conditions: a less "modern", less sophisticated form means a lower price and, consequently, an extension into a broader social clientele.[4]

In women's magazines, their constant renewal and search for variety is related to consumption, based on the principle of obsolescence and the "dynamism' of newness. This cult of the ephemeral reveals the essence of modernity, but as a class strategy: this periodic system of renewal, which in most cases is no more than a simple readjustment of units which themselves remain unchanged, is rich in mythical significance. Like fashion, it becomes a social practice; like fashion it reveals the coercive nature of modernity: what's being worn, what you must wear, what you must no longer wear. In women's magazines, daily life is organised in a repressive way, by the persuasive ideology of consumption, by advertising, which is simply the rhetoric of modernity. Indeed, all the objects which fill the consuming universe of these magazines reveal the co-existence of two levels: a practical level, an instrumental presence, and a symbolic level, whose implicit aim is to feign status or prestige. Although the use-function of the objects is accessory or artificial, their mythic function is real; they manifest "modernity"; they advertise their own ideology and thus close the circle. Women are imprisoned within the symbols of modernity, just as they were imprisoned, not long ago, within the symbols of the bourgeoisie: piano lessons and education in convent schools.

General aspects of the myth

We have rapidly surveyed this process of dilution of change brought about by the ideology of modernity, basing ourselves principally on women's publications. We were able to emphasise that in reality there are a great many examples which illustrate the thesis that modernity simply reiterates the structural elements of the system while giving them a fresh look. Now our intention is to refine the definition of modernity diffused by the consumer society, which advertises objects and types of behaviour, and shapes a style and a culture.

Modernity can be found in various compartmentalised areas, as we suggested in the previous section: urbanism, architecture, interior decoration, commercial art, writing, economic development, etc., areas which all operate around an implicit model of organisation of social relations. Each of these specific fields is significant of a virtual participation of the different social groups in cultural production, and thus in a general way in the determination of historical progress. Anticipating a more exhaustive analysis of the concept of modernity, we will define this *participation* as being restricted to the consumption of forms, devised and imposed by an emitter who influences the culture and the process of development of the dependent society. We shall locate this participation within the superstructure which creates "modern" aspirations directed towards a model of economic development subordinated to the dynamic demands of the economy of the metropolis, and creates a culture which will serve as a basis of implementation for this universalised model of society. We will try to detect the major lines of this strategy which imports symbols which are in tune with this project of development. *Beyond the objective qualities of modernity*, we will try to detach it from its innocent façade, its banal justification, its way of inserting itself in the order of things, where it corresponds to a supposedly "natural" notion of progress.

Modernity crystallises such apparently unrelated qualities as healthiness, beauty, rationality, freedom, confidence, originality, the avant-garde and the *unsurpassable, which nonetheless is constantly being surpassed*. These qualities achieve coherence through their integration into the notions of progress and victory over the unhealthy and the primitive, ideas which are proposed as the luminous, indisputable goal of a certain process of speculation on the future of humankind, the end of all alternatives.

In fact, nothing is more unstable than an integral definition of "the modern", nothing more difficult to establish than an inventory of its components. Whereas modernity should logically be *stabilised*, after resolving, perfecting and incorporating the characteristics which are supposed to compose it, and whereas the notion of modernity vindicates permanence, its concrete examples have, rather than stability, an accelerated rhythm of *death*. They are constantly being replaced by newer ones and relegated to the past tense. *Obsolescence* always goes along with modernity, and the tension between them reveals their essential equivalence with the false dynamism of a commercial circuit and the deceptive movement of a closed world. Every day or every season something new appears to replace its predecessor, sometimes exactly the same object presented in a more attractive wrapper, which, being moderately metamorphosed, supplants for a while its former appearance, now an object of derision. Remember: "An article which will keep you informed on today's makeup and make you laugh about what they said yesterday". It is thus easy to show that this false eternity of modernity corresponds in the most narrow way possible to the primordial need for consumption; its newness is that of the showcase, the coercive phosphorescence of the "latest thing" which hides, beneath sensationalism, the code of a class.

It is this same spectacularity which allows what is really no more than *repetitive banality* to become a source of constant information. The system reproduces itself exactly, but all the while removing its anecdotal signs. On this level, the system appears as a sequence which is always open. The symbols which pay tribute to the same order are repeated, but each time their surface is brought up to date.

Rejuvenation of appearances. The permanent essence remains intact. The notion of change allowed by modernity is graphically expressed in clothing, the packaging of which undergoes constant modifications in order to unleash and satisfy new libidinal and aesthetic needs and incorporate new techniques and materials. Appearance becomes a guiding principle to the extent to which it sets the very limits of change and the presentation of information about the world.

In this order of ideas, a question might be enlightening: what is a modern factory? Automatically a series of images come to mind, in an apparently disorderly parade: assembly lines with an accelerated work rhythm – an indication of successful output – guaranteed health conditions, a cheerful and airy canteen, colourful overalls, executive offices resembling the hotels and airports which are part of soaring international progress. No one would think to wonder about the relations between the boss, or rather the technostructure, and the workers in the factory. The modern factory can conceal a system of production and social relations which are a part of an intangible and atemporal order. But this will not cause modernity to lose its value, if the objection should be raised, since modernity develops essentially outside the concrete sphere of social relations.

The democracy of desires

Modernity has its own particular way of entering the world of the individual. It is presented as a cheerful, colourful, healthy formula for life, which transcends routine and in which conflicts are resolved the way acne is cured. The objects, clothing, fetishes, artefacts, in which our desires converge, are constantly being renewed in this rhetorical order which values the new for the mere fact of being new. And since on a technical level the new is implicitly a symbol of progress, the incitement is continually legitimised and regenerated.

Supported by the whole news and advertising apparatus, modernity intimately penetrates everyday life, mobilises the perceptive possibilities of the individual and appeals to the accessibility of all his or her senses through visual, audible and sensual references. The images projected by women's magazines, posters, TV programmes, shop windows, neon signs and all the other advertising methods – whose maximum efficiency is achieved through this convergence of stimuli – unleash the object's existence, its mental, psychic or neurotic incorporation into the experience of the individual. On the level of desire, technology embraces all of everyday life; contact with modernity is democratic. The universe of mass information which fosters the imaginary state of things does not segregate its audience. But the phenomenon, at the moment of acquisition, assumes a private aspect. Formal democracy thus comes up against the hardest reality: that of purchasing power and frustration.

Nonetheless, one cannot equate the relative openness of modernity with the variation of the phenomenon found in dependent countries. In the metropolitan countries, modernity has become a kind of watchword of standardised consumption, and the conformity of the clientele with the product allowed for this pseudo-universalising type. It was possible to create a common denominator on the basis of the indicators of prestige of a certain majority, a phenomenon which led Baudrillard[5] to state that "the international of prestige" has replaced the political international in the countries of the European Common Market. This uniformity has been carried over to the streets, where it creates an integration, superficial or not, of the masses. The most ostentatious differences between layers of society are erased in the metropolitan countries. In the street, the margin between the publicised reality of modernity and the reality of the consumer is allowed to persist, but it is accompanied by the possibility of participating in the same symbols. In fact, in every area in which it operates, modernity effects an artificial homogenisation of the appearance and image which the individuals themselves project. It acts as the superficial eraser of differences of status which clothing, for instance, would denote if this "image factory" did not exist.

In any case, in a dependent society, style appears, in the first analysis, as the privilege of an élite which, having developed certain forms, extends their use to a larger public (with a more commercial than paternalistic interest). Meanwhile, it regenerates its power of exclusivity by itself moving on to a new style. It is important to take note of these transfers of significance: the same style which originally conferred aristocracy, after a period of diffusion, confers democracy. At its peak, modernity is limited to the search for the distinctive signs of an élite and is sanctioned for its values of prohibitive consumption. In this sense, regional modernity does not faithfully reproduce the reality of the hegemonic countries, where the splendid objects sold in the Place Vendome or Fifth Avenue greatly surpass the semantic field of modernity, since they cannot be contained within a parameter of standardisation. In the regional capitals, there is no room for the Place Vendome, the Faubourg St Honoré or Fifth Avenue. Once an article has been established in a common pattern of consumption in the central economies, it is exported to dependent societies, where it in turn becomes élitist. This disbalance demonstrates the fact that when a product is imported, it is used in much more limited circles than those for whom it was originally intended. Nevertheless, through the process of "acclimatisation", this phenomenon is to a certain extent counteracted. In practice, the domestic economy contributes to the process of standardisation. The small workshops and part-time seamstresses who make up maxi-skirts, for example, and copy the basic lines of a fashion design, albeit imperfectly, take over an area which in the metropolitan economy would be an industrialised sector.

After a period of marked élitism, the democratisation of the signs of style causes them to lose their power of attraction for the hegemonic group. Moreover, such a standardisation would tend to give a dying image to the dominant class, implying its loss of the dynamics of newness. This class is thus obliged perpetually to feed the process of renovation in order to respond, in a dialectical movement, first to the commercial demands, which make them promote the democratic phase of style, and second, to the symbolic demands, which require a constant replenishment of their reserve of exclusive goods and models. It is this dialectical movement which established democratisation as the strategy of a class and as the expression of its false consciousness, since, in vulgarising "its" style, it hurries to leave the scene in search of another bit of tinsel which will revitalise its avant-garde privilege.

The democracy of themes

"In *Paula* this week:
- The loveliest Chilean weavings photographed in the countryside.
- How you yourself can lacquer your furniture and paint your house! A complete chart of modern colours which can give new life to any surroundings.
- How you can transform an old room into a cozy, dual-atmosphere apartment.
- A dramatic report on the daily tragedy experienced by the wives of the unemployed.
- *Paula* was there: the fashion festival organised by the Christmas Committee.
- And an indispensable guide for any home-maker: the ABC of First Aid."

Another phenomenon of dilution of those elements which the system cannot contain, and their recuperation into the cohesion of the myth, is that which we shall call "syncretism". All types of content and information are present, or at least represented in, the publications, responding to the need to satisfy the widest variety of interests. We therefore find the frivolous side-by-side with the important, the mundane with the political, sentimental anecdotes with cooking, children with gardening, and, in another sense, the subversive with the reactionary. Nor does advertising shrink from this paradoxical contiguity, this appropriation of a linguistic register. This would be startling, were it not accompanied by an adulteration of the meaning and a draining of the power of certain words which are genuinely alien to the ideological sphere of these magazines. As the slogan for *Eva* magazine says: "*Eva* has many reasons to be subversive."

The layout itself allows for this paradoxical contiguity. But the phenomenon of contiguity also permits a neutralisation of the potentially aggressive contents and a dilution of the revolutionary potential of certain informative articles: the news of an outburst of guerrilla violence is smothered by means of its juxtaposition with the announcement of the love affair of some prince. Moreover, the revolutionary content is itself neutralised by means of another phenomenon of dilution: the homogeneity of style. The rewriting of all the news leads to a particular style, characteristic of the genre, and which constitutes the supreme syncretism between the prosaic and the euphoric, through the use of various ruses, such as the use of a language dominated by a familiar, personalised tonality, an effusive and cozy tone. As Adorno pointed out, the more "massification" increases, and the more the technical-bureaucratic nature of the production of mass culture develops, "the more this ideology speaks to men with the sweet voice of the wolf disguised as Grandma".

One of the areas in which women's magazines exhibit a predilection for this syncretism is in interviews with more or less famous celebrities. Let us first make clear that in no way does this relative opening towards the outside world violate the universe of the magazines, since it always conforms to the magazine's code. An example of this is the fact that these articles systematically give preference to show business personalities: singers, actors, etc. Any violations of the established order which could be attributed to this would-be vanguard are minimised, since the dominant ideology is careful to isolate such people in a special category, that of the *enfant terrible*. Their productions (even when subversive) can be enjoyed as part of "culture", stripped of any relation with the political. It is significant, in addition, that the people chosen are only able to cross the threshold of women's magazines when they have already achieved recognition elsewhere, and when their appearance guarantees sensationalism.

The magazines appropriate their names and prestige, but never contribute to their discovery. Ironically, this universe, obsessed by novelty, only pays tribute to the new when it has already passed the inspection of the general audience, and when the message radiated by this newness is ready to be adopted as one of the cultural categories of the bourgeoisie.

Let's take the example of an interview, published in *Paula*, with a person known for expressing values subversive of the social order, and devoid of political ambiguity: protest singer Victor Jara:[6] "But today he is already a winner. His latest LP for the Discoteca del Canto Popular, DICAP, has had a fabulous success. Its title is "Canto Libre" [Song of Freedom], but it is no longer really protest music . . ." Olympian nature is thus the first credential. The second, always revealed as a discovery during the course of the conversation, is the *Man*. In this particular example, a mixture of humanity and domesticity is highlighted. The expression of the life experience of the individual – mediated by the interview – infallibly revolves around the significant landmarks of women's magazines: "He talks to *Paula* about love and women, about his life and dreams, his work and ideals". If the person is harder to integrate and offers more resistance to the mechanisms of mimicry, the solution is to make use of this very resistance and emphasise the natural and irremediable distance between the world of the magazine and the Olympian rebel, seen as an incidental object of consumption. A preliminary reserve is established: between him and *us* there is a barrier. His universe is a whole (separate from ours), a popular whole, the origin of which explains the political motivation and the rebellious dimension of the repertoire. "A troubadour who sings to his people." The two worlds are defined as exact parallels. His *being of the people* explains his *singing for the people*, and defines and limits the personal logic of a life, the authenticity of Victor Jara, ruling out any possible explanation beyond that determined by the magazine as "natural".

A certain amazement is evident on the part of the magazine upon realising that Another Order can be sung about and longed for by someone who, although different from themselves, yet possesses qualities on which they believed they had a monopoly. "This rough man, with his Indian features . . . conceals a tenderness which is hard to resist. After talking to him for a while, it is hard to believe that he is the author of those stinging songs. On the other hand, we understand those other songs, those full of poetry, a better reflection of the Victor Jara we met." In virtue of this supposed split between two alternatives of a personality, the recuperation of the rebellious entity is made possible, as well as his incorporation into more acceptable, assimilable categories. This fear of the *whole man* reveals the purely artificial nature of syncretism, and of the obvious farce when women's magazines try to surpass the fragmentation of their informational and referential universe.

At this point, we also cannot pass up the opportunity to emphasise a very deep, significant omission made by women's magazines. It is the way in which the presentation of "history" necessarily amputates those events called "political".

"During the ten years of *Vanidades*, incredible things have happened: man has gone to the moon, transplanted hearts, accomplished great changes in art, literature, cinema, fashion, youth. All of these have been gathered into this special anniversary issue."

The magazine's way of cutting out events from the Large Outside, the exterior world, conforms exactly to the criteria of the Small Order of the magazine, and responds to the demands of intimacy, spectacularity and sensationalism.

The "dehistoricisation" of this world forces it to look towards naturalness for a perpetual reference of values. "The genuinely natural line." There is a need to be forgiven for the earlier refinement by putting the emphasis on naturalness, the guardian of simplicity and healthy morality. The more sophisticated and sumptuous the object, the greater the rhetorical reliance on naturalness and the return to nature. The new proves its worth by its approximation to the natural, and its goodness is asserted to the background of a fresh country scene in which romp the couple and the child, all luminous in the morning air: "Menth-O-Dent. They were right to call it new. The purified and purifying product." Alongside pottery from Pomaire, Chile, and handwoven blankets is displayed a New Line of elegance, with its accent on naturalness, innocently hiding the clearly foreign connotation of the latest brand of shoes being advertised: Royle.

By a process of sublimation, a form of life corresponding to concrete naturalness is done away with. Corresponding to the "rural" is a signifier deformed by the urban angle of vision, the photography appropriates the forms of poverty and simplicity, but not their content. Ahead of us, as we already mentioned, lies the spectacle of an abstract, touristic and anecdotal countryside. It serves as a foundation in a style which salvages from the wilds the traditional materials and forms, woollens, rustic weaving and basketry, bridging the gap between rural and urban life with a yearning to make naturalness the guardian angel of the consumer civilisation. And at the same time to emphasise and take advantage of the aesthetic values which such products acquire within the atmosphere of wealth and development of the city.

"For the starving man, it is not the human form of food that exists, but only its abstract being as food; it could just as well be there in its crudest form, and it would be impossible to say wherein this feeding-activity differs from that of *animals*. The care-burdened man in need has no sense for the finest play; the dealer in minerals sees only the mercantile values but not the beauty and the unique nature of the mineral: he has no mineralogical sense."[7]

Style and the cosmos

"This is the world of your security: Right Guard."
"Enter the dynamic world of Nescafé."
"The year's world-wide success! Golobo. Panties so wash-and-wear they'll take you round the globe!"

In the advertising jargon of fashion, there is invariably a reference to the "world", the product becoming the centre of a universe which seems to expand until it has the dimensions of the globe and in this way emancipates all its consumers. Simultaneously, it creates a community around itself. Behind an apparent openness, which would seem to imply the acceptance of a certain anonymity, intimate tendencies surface. The product becomes the new way to fight against isolation and repel the unknown and the strange. This corresponds exactly to the order which regulates women's magazines and which they in turn promote and advertise: the world of the home, the world of women, the world of youth. Like the consumers' "clan" which triumphantly enters the new and spectacular Braniff ad: "The Clan says: Let's end the farce. Let's make a Crediclan and it's done, overnight! Now, we'll arrange for plane tickets, hotel rooms, trips and car rentals. Down with bureaucracy, roared the Clan!" The Braniff Clan eliminated differences. Through objects and goods – they claim – is achieved the integration which liberates the individual and his power of decision, giving him at last the right to speak out and discover the world.

The world of the object? It is the realisation of Utopia. No need for change. Your happiness is right here. Our daily coffee or detergent will at last satisfy your desire to be yourself. They will fulfil your need to give your opinion, to be in command of your own experience. They will give you pleasure, freedom and fantasy, to you and to all those who can now share your good fortune. The consumers rise to power.

Another key element in advertising jargon is the grouping of the products, and therefore their beneficiaries, around the creative centres, the real promoters and exponents of consumption: "Paris, New York, London, Lux soap preferred by all". "The fabrics with the same modern patterns which were the rage in Europe last season." The acquisition of these goods, invested with the magnificence radiated by such capitals, brings to life the mythical participation in the lifestyles and images of the upper regions of the developed world, which concede a little of their exclusivity and fortune with every new design. And this same incentive is repeated in dependent countries, where the modernist model, through ritual acts of consumption, symbolically gratifies the desire for integration into the society which generated it.

In the intellectual domain, we find a strikingly identical phenomenon. Cultural references in advertising revolve around the "best sellers", regardless of the object's place in the hierarchy of cultural productions. The only criteria used are sales, prestige, controlled good taste, and the indispensable style. Before going on to examples, however, let us note that advertising only penetrates the category of culture in order to disguise the colonisation to which it contributes, limited to the domestic sphere. Advertising seeks to situate the object within the noble chain of the power of the immaterial (relative immateriality, however, contaminated with immediacy by its consecration as an object of fashion):

"My favourite books range from Normal Mailer to Marcuse and McLuhan. But don't get me wrong. I also love the incredible adventures of Fleming's James Bond . . . I am a woman of my time in every way, and that's why I also dress in modern, practical clothes . . . like my Dunova sweater set."

The ellipsis is not ours. It constitutes the pause needed before closing this example of modern eclecticism.

We should now highlight the mechanism of inversion operating in this integrationist strategy, by virtue of which advertising has become an ideological form. A qualitative transfer is produced between the subject and the object. The inanimate world (things, objects) becomes animated, while in an exact parallel, the animate world loses its animation. To a humanised object there corresponds a reified being. And if this being manages to recover its quality, movement, dynamism and personality, it is through the mediation of the object. The sense of value is found not in the being, but in the thing.

The relationship between individuals is thus transformed through the introduction of the product, and through technical and commercial innovations: "Me . . . You . . . Airomint." Graphically, the pre-eminent object, the mouthwash, is inserted between the two faces of a couple and encourages their meeting, taking priority over the quality of love. Moreover, there can be seen a constant wavering between the semantic field of emotion, on the one hand, and of the object on the other. The mouthwash "guarantees clean speech", "Airominted breath" contributes to the purity of the couple. In this constant transposition, you no longer know who is who. Love and sensuality are crystallised in socks or lipsticks, promoted to the ranks of essential actors. The human-to-human relationship disappears, with the resurgence of the human-object couple, which seems to satisfy them in a much more effective and less painful way. The object is integrated in the individual sphere, evidently making use of the frustrations felt by the consuming entity in the domain of interpersonal and sexual relations. It proposes a compensation for the complexity and hardness of the world.

"Fabiola Pantyhose are adorably smooth. They tenderly hug your leg." Durability is transformed into fidelity, proximity to the skin into sensuality, silky fibre into caresses and affection. Fidelity, tenderness, smoothness, sensuality, an intimate comprehension of the desire for liberation: the object replaces the best lover and moves into the centre of the narcissistic relationship one has with oneself. Thus, through the world of the object, and in the democratised and standardised context of consumption, the mythology of the good and bad genies, is now recreated, and a magic universe is staked out beneath the efficient and rational surface of modernity. "In order to hear this message integrally, you have to give up the idea that we have entered rational societies (called industrial) from which magic and utopias vanished a long time ago and where only ideology lingers a while before disappearing."[8]

In response to our last observations, someone might object that advertising is an autonomous area and that the meanings which we have discovered and pointed out may not be valid outside this limited sphere. But this objection fades in the light of a global examination of these publications: the mechanism of reduction of reality operates throughout the many areas, whose fragmentation confers a mosaic quality on women's magazines. The advertising language which makes the object the mediator of relationships both between the individual and him/herself and the individual and others is only reflecting a constant of the language of modernity which evades an unsteady, deep and conflicting reality, to the benefit of the false harmony of the object.

Gradually, the power of the object proceeds, through a simplistic but subtly disguised escalation, towards an apotheosis. In this is revealing:

"Black Power," it says, "has come to feminine beauty. After the violence of the streets and the black liberation literature, the cult of blackness has arrived in the lighter, frivolous world of cosmetics . . . Until now, the world of cosmetics has always looked to the white woman for inspiration. This is what is changing."

Black Power could not remain outside the myth of universality. The eternally feminine will allow for the recuperation of the most subversive elements. Angela Davis' rivals do not escape the natural condition of women; class struggle, supported by demands for racial equality, is transformed into an innocent phenomenon of beauty contests. Helped by those myths which turn secondary and accessory values into essential ones, segregations are absorbed and conflicts disarmed. The object, cosmetics, universalises, integrates and levels off all the contradictions.

We have had several opportunities to look at the way in which the culture of modernity approaches the individual and creeps into his conscious and subconscious life. Among the preferred forms in the strategy of advertising, we should take special note of the most obvious: the mythical incentive, newness, is given emphatic value through the graphic solution of capital letters: NEW LINE. This form, corresponding to the sudden triumphant rise of the tone of voice in broadcasting, is indicative of the affirmative character assumed by modernity within consumer society's global cultural project. This is the same holy terror – constituting a fundamental aspect of communication in our societies – to which Marcuse refers, speaking of affirmative culture or closed discourse. Morin, on the other hand, in a humouristic tone, takes part in tracking down the repressive forms which have their source in the communication phenomenon, interpreting advertising language as a "meta national anthem."

As Morin clearly shows, modernity occupies the centre of the duality – inherent in the advertising message – between information and incitement, to the extent that its "signifiers", or concrete supports, cover the global field of temptations, while its "signified" is equipped with the notions of dynamism, change and irreversible progress. In other words, modernity is the formula for the opening of the consumer world towards the future, characterised by the rhetoric of fantasy, which hides the essential fact that the theme of newness only plays back the deceptive myths of bourgeois culture and ensures the perpetuation of the process of dependency. Modernity allows the technocratic society to stimulate the alliance with liberating ideologies. Responding to a strategy of consumer massification, it tries to eliminate the sign of the act which it propitiates, by offering itself as a way of integration into the ideology of harmony, health and happiness. It tends to make one forget that the compulsion of consumption which unleashes deeply selfish forces, in its search for a temporary pleasure in buying, makes the consumer a prisoner. Through modernity, the act of consumption disappears as a cultural act which contributes to developing an individualistic and repressive civilisation.

As we have seen, woman is at the centre of this strategy for action. Through her, all the emancipating postulates of modernity are revealed, and through her, as we have emphasised, they are all absorbed. The institutional basis of her status and her participation in the production of goods remains unscathed. Marriage, the family, the controlled disbalance between the rôles and the authorities, come forth as the elements of the order whose static nature must be recognised in order to establish the norms of the harmony – always precarious, but ceaselessly desired – within the very walls of the cage. Normality continues to be defined in relation to an untouched order and an intangible legality. Now, as we have noted, women, limited and held down in this way, are the centre of the everyday world. Through women's temporality, a quality of life and reality is attained, a whole atmosphere is created, a dimension of culture which is engraved in daily gestures.

The liberation of Eros is inscribed, likewise, within the emancipating self-definition of modernity. The consumer culture is undoubtedly nourished by this source of desire, disturbance, prohibition and frustration which sex continues to signify. Yet a key question emerges: Eros unchained or Eros chained? Answer: Eros, unchained, chained. The structure of motivations of which consumption is a part confuses sex with the elements of social success and access to the sphere of money and material well-being. As a model of liberation it offers the images of the advertising cover girls, neutered and antiseptic. Sex has become an aesthetic-playful motif, rendered banal and stripped of both the dazzling nature of Eros and its cursed and painful aspects. Modernity continues to envisage sexuality as a compensation, the counterpoint of work, the source of leisure which rewards a life organised in such a way that the reality principle contradicts the pleasure principle, a life centred on the acquisition of goods which standardise and isolate, turning the individual away from the search for pleasure and mobilising his or her instinctive energy towards goals other than those of Eros, as a possibility for real communication and immersion in the community. Fashion, for instance, constitutes the alibi of sexuality, a provocative and insolent alibi, certainly, but never the expression of the liberation of Eros; styles are the index of an exceedingly demanding submission to the imperatives of the social code which dissolves pleasure in a narcissistic satisfaction and mundane enjoyment, and sublimates it to the level of conformity with the conventions of a social milieu.

Did you ever see the poster by the Cuban artist Fremez, where he sets the faces of two women against one another? One is the profile of a vamp, who is painting her mouth with a red lipstick, a very, very bright red – a red which, on the face of the Vietnamese woman next to her, becomes blood.

Part Three

Crises

1: The media and revolutionary crisis: the Chilean experience

Despite the essential place accorded to it by Trotsky, and more importantly Gramsci, the question of information and everyday life during a period of revolution has not generally been on the immediate agenda when progressive forces achieve political power. In fact, the most recent experiences have tended to show that when this question *is* posed, the Left seems incapable of answering.

Some analysts of the Chilean drama have seen this deficiency as one of the causes of the rout of 11 September 1973. In effect, the press, television and radio were powerful tools in the hands of the bourgeoisie, who mobilised vast sectors of the population against the socialist experiment. Yet the Chilean case remains one of the most profitable lessons of history. It reminds us that information is a political issue and, as such, is important for the recovery of power (as well as for establishing a new order). In this respect it is useful to go through the ups and downs of the Chilean experiment.

Official documents have disclosed the financial assistance given by the United States' Central Intelligence Agency to the campaigns of agitation launched by the Chilean bourgeoisie against the government of Salvador Allende and Popular Unity. This enabled the information media to take over from the campaigns of intimidation with which the population had been inundated during the electoral period. These subsidies also helped it to compensate for a drop in advertising receipts, whilst at the same time those multinational advertising agencies remaining in Santiago put their services at the disposal of a campaign of unrest and propaganda.

The first reaction to the Allende government was the creation of a veritable information deluge, both through the launching of new publications and an intensified importing of American magazines and television series, whose ideology was not exactly impregnated with revolutionary ideas. Respect for the free flow of information, observed from first to last by the Allende government, also forbade it to impose limits on this invasion. On television Channel 13, controlled by the conservative parties, for example, American material increased from forty per cent to seventy per cent. Five publications were launched for young people, two of which remained chronically in deficit but were nonetheless sustained by the Right – in violation of the "law of the market", the centrepiece of its credibility.

The struggle against the proposed nationalisation of the newsprint industry was in turn led by *El Mercurio*, the largest national daily, and itself linked body and soul to the newsprint monopoly. In so doing, it laid bare the hidden reality of press freedom. The Right both stocked the paper and organised the sabotage of its distribution.[1]

Nor could Popular Unity do anything against those big international news agencies which remained in Chile. Its own newspapers continued to a large extent to depend on them for international information. After a defamatory campaign against Allende, however, United Press International (UPI) was closed by the government, but the outcry (in the name of freedom of expression) was such that the ban had to be lifted two days later. The method is familiar in press campaigns against progressive regimes: accusations appear more "objective" when launched outside before being parachuted into the country in question. ITT had already come up with this idea, as revealed in documents that fell into the hands of the US Senate, and it has since gained widespread acceptance. Such strategies of ideological isolation show how thin is the margin for manoeuvre by regimes threatening the interests of the hegemonic classes or multinational corporations. They also show that freedom of expression needs to be defined in terms of both internal and external power relations.

This does not, in itself, explain why the Right was able to dominate the terrain of the media. After its defeat at the ballot box in September 1970, the conservative press launched disruptive campaigns which failed to clarify their targets. However, from the beginning of 1972 and the re-cementing of the coalition between the Christian Democrats and the traditional Right (National Party), the opposition forces radically changed their model of the press in terms of the political alliances formed to offer resistance to the Popular Unity government. The consumer of information was no longer to be the passive reader familiar from periods of bourgeois normality: from then on, he or she was targeted as the doctor who went on strike, the woman who left her household to protest in the streets, and the blockading trucker who paralysed the transport system.[2]

The press campaigns of the Right were aimed specifically at the professional associations and corporate bodies of the *petit bourgeoisie*; and they stood by these "mass fronts" in their strikes. The "liberal" press became a channel for the organisation of the disillusioned, a tribune for the "silent majority" (which, having had reason to believe that it had finally been given the floor, would experience a rude awakening on the morning after the *coup d'état*). No longer content simply to inform, the press called on its readers to combat the government. *El Mercurio*, which until three years before liked to present itself as *The Times* of Latin America, transformed itself into a popular manifesto, dramatically changing its style, the traditional balance of its headlines and, of course, its editorial content. Just as the employers' associations went beyond their normal limits during the large-scale strikes, so the newspapers and journalists went beyond their accepted boundaries and formed a determined vanguard in the counter-revolution.

When one turns to the position of the Left, one can only wonder why information is customarily relegated to be one of the minor arts of revolutionary war. We can only too readily recognise here the ravages of an economist approach which, with or without its theoretical finery, gives priority in changing society to the overthrowing of the economic order, itself expected to trigger off revolutionary innovation in the cultural arena. The undervaluing of the ideological field stems from these currents of thought and practice.

Behind economist dogma shelters a particular conception of the whole state apparatus and the levers needed to change its class character. In the area of mass communications, the mainstream Left has too often been content to try to "democratise" the existing set-up, avoiding any questioning of the social relations regulating the means of production of information and culture. In the face of conservative forces which, in order to reaffirm their hegemony, did not hesitate to breach the principles underlying the organisation of their media, the Left fell, in this area as in others, into the trap of playing to rules not of its own making.

The principal mistake of Popular Unity was not to have clearly defined a policy of alliances. This weakness was all the more serious in the field of information, in that day after day it had to address various audiences beyond its natural allies and swim against the tide of the cultural heritage of "normal" everyday life in a capitalist society.

In a combat unequally balanced from the outset, the Chilean Left was always in control of less ammunition than the Right. Out of sixty-four newspapers and 134 radio stations (the most influential medium in a country like Chile), only ten newspapers and thirty-six radio stations supported the government. No media were expropriated by the Left, which limited itself to buying up a handful of companies. Within the newspapers controlled by the right, certain forms of struggle nevertheless took shape. After six months of argument within the newspaper *El Mercurio*, the left-wing leadership of the union was dismissed and, by the use of "legal" stratagems, the monolithic cohesion of the right was restored. In some provincial dailies, printing workers went as far as to obtain the right to express their own interpretation of events underneath editorials which reflected the ideas of the management. They thus revived a form of struggle inaugurated by the Cuban revolutionaries at a time when, after the fall of Batista, they were not yet totally in control.

So far as television was concerned, the authority of Popular Unity over the national channel was in practice considerably lessened by the continuation of personnel appointed by the previous Christian-Democrat administration. A law passed during the presidency of Frei ensured that they could not be removed. Even the union remained in the hands of the Christian Democrats. Furthermore, the phenomenal difference between the cost of relaying programmes produced in the United States and the cost of national programmes (up to twenty times more expensive), strongly reduced the possibilities for the left. The habits and tastes created among the public by the established model of television made themselves felt with all their force. American series retained the largest audiences: when a series like *The FBI* appeared on television, it gained seventy-two per cent of the audience. Channels favourable to the government obtained the highest audiences only when they presented programmes of this type, which they used as bait to try to win the battle for hearts and minds.

The state publishing house Quimantu, created after the takeover of a firm which had gone bankrupt, was considered as the uncontested kingdom of the Left in publishing. But here again the situation was paradoxical: by virtue of contract clauses, Quimantu had to use the state presses to print magazines like *Reader's Digest* and Walt Disney comics – which it then proceeded to attack in its own publications. Many on the Left preferred to carry on the ideological struggle separately in organs of information and cultural institutions under their own control. But a grouping of left-wing journalists, created in the enthusiasm of the electoral victory and bringing together information professionals of the Left and Far-Left, never succeeded in getting off the ground.

However, within the state publishing house, a strategy approved by the parties making up the Popular Unity coalition *was* able to express itself. This orientation could also be found with variations on Channel 9 of the University of Chile and on the national Channel 7, two other areas where the Left attempted to legitimise its public presentation. This policy was deployed in two directions. Firstly, by "democratising" access to works of national and foreign literature –

in two and a half years, five million books were published in popular editions, twice as many as were distributed in Chile during the seventy previous years. And, secondly, by using genres and styles made familiar by the cultural industries, such as news magazines, comics, photo-novels and sports magazines, to initiate a re-orientation of the "ideology of the middle classes" and open up these genres to new values.

But the degree of radicalisation easily attained by class struggle did not allow this progressive strategy to bear fruit. The Left carried out a policy of social "pacification" so as not to scare the middle classes by an over-dramatic polarisation, whilst the Right was already agitating in the streets. Whereas the conservative forces addressed these classes with a language of mobilisation and anchored their approach in the everyday reality of their component groups, appealing to particular interests, the Left seemed to address itself to an indistinct whole, taking on board the amorphous notion of "public opinion". The irreproachable position of the Popular Unity government, respectful to the last of liberal pluralism, did not, however, protect it from accusations of indoctrination and brain-washing.

Did a new type of information emerge in the Chile of Allende? Some initiatives did emerge from party research units, journalists and intellectuals, putting into practice a "pedagogical" approach to news and analysis in weeklies like *Chile Hoy*. Above all, through the popular organisations which emerged in October 1972 in reaction to the rightist offensive, numerous newspapers appeared, produced by workers with the help of militant journalists and known as the press of "the industrial belts".

After the employers' general strike at the end of October, 1972, the workers in the outskirts of Santiago and some provincial towns began to form *cordones industriales* in response to the growing bourgeois offensive. As a result of rank-and-file initiative, these soon became embryos of popular power, organs of direct democracy around which the working class began to mobilise and organise itself. In the same way, workers throughout this intensification of the mass movement began to develop new means of disseminating information. These popular newspapers had their counterpart in several brief pro-grammes on the national television channel and the entire program-ming of the channel of the University of Chile during the last six months of the regime, when it opened itself up completely to the dynamic of the workers' movement. Although remaining at an embryonic stage, these newspapers and programmes nevertheless testified to the beginnings of dual power within this section of the state apparatus.

The actions of an October bourgeoisie

Most studies have looked at the operation of the dominant communications system in periods of normality. What becomes of this system at times of social conflict has rarely been examined. Such disruption, which introduces politicisation and mobilisation into structures by definition "demobilising", also speaks volumes about the normal functioning of the liberal order.[3]

October 1972 marked the peak of the period of revolutionary high tension experienced by Chile between 1972 and 1973. In that month, the bourgeoisie played its trump card in a test of strength. Hostilities began on the eleventh with the proclamation of an unlimited strike by the association of road transporters, who sought in theory to show their opposition to a government plan to form a national road transport company in the south of the country. In the days that followed, all the professional organisations of the "middle class" joined the strike. Against this attempt to paralyse the country, the popular movement mobilised to ensure the maintenance of production and supplies, and to organise security against an increase in violent incidents, evidence of the insurrectional intentions of the bourgeoisie. A great moment in the history of the workers' movement, October 1972 involved complete transformations in people's ways of thinking, new forms of organisation and the smashing of traditional hierarchies. The Chilean October was in some ways a response to the Paris Commune. However, it was also the most intense moment of bourgeois resistance to Popular Unity.

There is also no doubt that from 1970 to October 1972, the media was the favoured launching pad for the bourgeois offensive. Although there were differences of emphasis and sometimes even important contradictions, the media in the hands of the various sectors of the Right had manifestly unified itself behind the ideological campaigns against the popular government. This unification and convergence became more obvious and more efficient in times of crisis, as October 1972 showed. The war unleashed by the bourgeoisie directed all its artillery against the government forces through its newspapers, its radio stations and – even more strangely – its television channel – Channel 13 of the Catholic University of Santiago – one of the most effective sniping points. And if newspapers and radio stations were able to assume the rôle of rallying and mobilising increasingly large sectors of the *petit bourgeoisie*, this was because previously, without interruption, they were both engaged in defending these sectors. This aspect constituted, without doubt, the central point of the campaign to influence public opinion launched by the bourgeoisie through its information systems. Thus, the more it enlarged its social support base, the better it clouded its real class interests by making them appear to be those of the "majority".

The established methods of communication normally consist – when the dominant classes control the whole state apparatus – in reproducing the codes, values and norms of the system as so many natural responses which tend to justify the existing order of things. But what becomes of that rôle when the bourgeoisie, no longer in government, passes into opposition? The clash between the values and interests it defends and the new order trying to establish itself expresses in acute form the bypassing of all those liberal notions of free expression, free-flow, objectivity and public opinion.

The deepening of class contradictions, brought about by the measures of the popular government, resulted in an increasing trend for the means of communication controlled by the bourgeoisie to become openly more and more fascist. The need to nourish this "front" to win the political battle was to lead to the destruction of the sacrosanct notion of objectivity, at the same time as the need to defend "its" freedom of expression was reinforced. It is only a small step between the will to exercise this freedom and a justification for the freedom of seditious agitation. In simplified terms, it was in these margins that the ideological battle was carried out. And from its rôle as leader of public opinion, the bourgeois apparatus of mass communication transformed itself into a leader of "corporatist power".[4]

Opposition MPs quickly recognised the importance of the rôle played by the information media during the employers' strike and hailed its efficiency. Accusing the Confederation of Democratic Parties (a bloc made up from the traditional Right and the Christian Democrats) of lacking political direction and arguing that this lack had caused a "serious power vacuum", they emphasised the rôle of journalists:

"A group of eminent journalists has filled this vacuum and succeeded in orienting public opinion. In the face of the changes in policy demanded by the country, the Democratic Confederation has often abdicated its responsibilities. It has been in their places of employment that individuals have made their protests – and thanks to their various corporations."[5]

From informed citizen to man of action

This turbulence – recognisably profitable from a political point of view – emanating from the information media, contributed in practice to the complete overthrow of the normal running of everyday life. In the framework of the general crisis, everyone witnessed the micro-crisis of the means of communication. The media, normally seen as technical and neutral, became veritable actors in the crisis. There were thirteen days in which the national radio chain was brought under the direct control of the government information department; there were special editions of the newspapers *La Prensa* (Christian Democrat daily) and *El Siglo* (the Communist daily); *Teletrece* (evening news broadcast on the Catholic University channel) was expanded to two hours, a record length for a televised news programme; and there was the transmission of last-minute news in the middle of an immensely popular American spy series, *Mission Impossible*. Finally, the various radio stations of the opposition "opted out" of the compulsory national network and transmitted home-made shows produced to celebrate "the saga of freedom . . ."

The main spokespersons of the opposition parties hastened to emphasise the lack of orchestration and the spontaneity of this movement of insurrection. *El Mercurio*, the biggest national daily, and an illustrious example of the liberal press in Latin America, became, during the October crisis, the ventriloquist of the "Democratic Confederation" and insisted on this lack of orchestration. Nevertheless, the unity with which the communications front of the opposition had burst into action became increasingly transparent. One common feature was the use of a rhetoric until then limited to the sensationalist press. Differences between the various journalistic genres – that social division of labour which operates between press organs destined for very diverse clienteles in periods of liberal normality – were reduced. Wiping out former differences, newspapers united under the banner of furthering the agitation, testifying to a great deal of mutual support. They thus sought to organise the human potential liberated by the strike.

Unity, orchestration, solidarity. To these elements we should add another which characterises even more closely the very nature of information: the "practical character" of the messages put into circulation. This aspect synthesises completely the rupture signified by the October crisis in relation to traditional liberal practice, and it was essentially present at three levels. First, the newspaper became a means of contact between "corporations", a link between the agents and the bases of sedition through the extensive column inches devoted to pro-strike press releases from various sectors. These press releases multiplied, and among the most prominent for their length, their regularity and their virulence were those of *Poder Femenino* (Women's Power).[6] Second, the choice of news and front page headlines identified the newspaper as a public relations agent for the strikers, celebrating the unilateral advance of the crisis: the paralysing of the country, bypassing of the constitutional authorities, a vacuum of authority, the disruption of democratic co-existence. Finally, in its function of "organic intellectual" for the strike movement, the newspaper enounced in its editorials the basic ideas and principles of action recommended for the Democratic Confederation and, above all, the employers' associations – the national organisation of large landowners (SNA) and the national association of manufacturers (SOFOFA) – the real headquarters of the crisis.

These newspapers were not alone in calling for concrete political action. By virtue of their capacity for mobilisation through the rapidity with which they diffuse information, radio (and television) went much further. Until their closure by the government's declaration of a state of emergency, radio stations helped organise civil resistance in different areas – for example, telling women in residential areas where to buy flour at a given moment.

To better understand this new strategy of the Right, we should remember the implicit division on which the ideological struggle is normally based. When the hegemony of the dominant classes is not threatened, a hiatus is implicitly programmed by the liberal bourgeois press between information and action. Its fundamental objective is thereby the demobilisation and disorganisation of the masses (to better organise them around the values of the dominant classes). It speaks to the individual man/woman, separated from his/her class, to public opinion seen as the sum of isolated false consciousnesses, a "silent majority" which supports and tacitly reproduces its system of domination.

When its interests are threatened, the bourgeoisie needs to mobilise opinion for the defence of its class. The tacit agreement of its clientele is no longer enough. A change then occurs in the notion of the audience. From the reader-consumer we arrive at the reader-man of action, able to defend class interests through active resistance. This implies a second modification in the image of the audience: from the individual being, the isolated will, we arrive at the collective being. One of the most efficient mediators of this regrouping was to be the press, as an organiser and strategist of the popular fronts of the bourgeois opposition.

As we shall see, the selection of news during the October crisis went through the axis constituted by the mass fronts, particularly through what was dubbed "corporatist power" (*poder gremial*). In newspapers, with the exception, however, of *La Prensa* (the Christian Democrat daily) where nuances intervened, the authority of "corporations" co-opted by the Right took over from political parties, which lost a good part of their media power of representation during the conflict.[7] It was only at the end of the conflict, when the aggression of the opposition forces decreased in the face of failure, that political parties regained their position as protagonists on the stage of information.[8]

A further point is worth making here about the importance accorded to the means of communication by the bourgeoisie. This is quite obviously the sector of its material hegemony where it can best dress up the defence of private property and social control with prestigious claims from the heritage of culture and democracy (freedom of expression, objectivity, pluralism). Studies on the ownership of the means of disseminating information in Chile have shown that the opposition forces had clear majority control over the media and have therefore argued that Chile was probably the only country in the world where pro-government forces had less access to public opinion than the opposition.

To the examples already given, let us add the following. The six nationally-distributed newspapers published by the Right were bought by 540,000 people daily, compared with 312,000 for the five left-wing dailies. The Right controlled forty-one of the sixty-one newspapers published in the provinces, whereas the Left controlled only eleven. The owners of these publications had close links with the National Party (formerly the Conservative Party) and the Christian Democrats, as well as with owners of large farms, industries and businesses. Of the 134 radio stations,[9] nearly a hundred belonged to the opposition. Moreover, the stations belonging to the Right were equipped with powerful transmitters which effectively made them into national networks. The most powerful of these stations (and those which were to play the most active rôle during the illegal strike of the truckers and shopkeepers) belonged to the Christian Democrats, the National Party and even the extreme-right movement, Fatherland and Liberty.

Apart from their alliances with the monopolist bourgeoisie, the opposition media benefited from another support. The "legality" of their activities was assured to a large extent by the "Statute of Constitutional Guarantees" signed by Salvador Allende before formally taking office. This was, among other things, the price he had to pay for his election being ratified by the Christian Democrats in parliament. Promulgated at the initiative of the Christian Democrats, this agreement accorded an exceptional status to the information media, which could only be nationalised by a special law. Thus was legal status given to the hegemony of the bourgeoisie, and a *carte blanche* for its future efforts at massive mobilisation against the popular government.

The "free radio" war

One of the numerous articles and editorials devoted by *El Mercurio* during October 1972 to the problem of the "threat" to freedom of expression also accurately presented the role adopted by right-wing radio stations during the employers' strike. The threatened closure of stations were interpreted thus:

"Reducing radio stations to silence through the illegal compulsory network ... corresponded to the vain intention to give an image of apparent normality and above all to the idea that by depriving the so-called minority of easy and rapid means of communication, it would be easy to discourage corporatists isolated in the provinces, or situated in workplaces distanced from one another in the same town..." *(El Mercurio, 29 October)*

Here, the goals and the significance of the dissemination of information are defined by those concerned: a means by which the command posts of the strike can keep in touch with their bases.

What also emerges is the solidarity deployed by the various communication groups, as much to make up for the silence imposed on some as to capitalise politically on this fact and call on the population to form a united front to defend the "freedom of expression" frozen by the popular government. Let us look at some of the important dates in the movement unleashed around the media during the crisis.

15 October

Despite three military announcements broadcast under the state of emergency forbidding "any disclosure and broadcasting of alarmist and tendentious information destined to influence public order", the station *Nuevo Mundo*, transmitting live from the headquarters of the Christian Democrat Party (where 600 militants were brought together by the management), called on its bases to "move into action". The military command of the region ordered the closure of the station for six days and at 21.30 hours it was closed down. On the recommendation of the military command, the government decreed the suspension of radio transmissions and the establishment of a single national network. This occurred at 21.55 hours.

At 22.30 hours, interrupting the normal course of the televised news on Channel 13, its manager, Father Hasbun, called on viewers to contribute to the campaign launched to spread this "objective and impartial channel" throughout the province, a channel henceforth "the voice of those reduced to silence" (a direct allusion to the setting up of a national radio network). This was a way of emphasising that

Channel 13 would take up the position of the opposition radios.

From this date onwards, the news broadcast of Channel 13 doubled in length and the morning daily *La Prensa* published a daily supplement at six in the evening.

18 October
On Channel 13 the programme *The Opposition Replies* was launched to respond to the intervention of President Allende, with the "pluralist" presence of four parliamentarians representing each of the opposition parties (National Party, Christian Democrats, Radicals of the Right and Radicals of the Left).

21 October
The launching, without seeking the necessary permission, of a new political programme on Channel 13. Entitled *Chile, Heritage and Destiny*, its sole aim was to offer a platform for ex-Presidents of the Republic (it was well-known that there were no left-wing presidents still alive). This innovation allowed Eduardo Frei (Christian Democrat, 1964–70) to speak that same day. On the 23rd, it was the turn of Gonzalez Videla (Radical Party, 1946–52, elected with the aid of Communist votes but who turned against the Communists in 1948 under the pressure of the Cold War, and set up concentration camps for them. The poet Pablo Neruda had to cross the Andes cordillera into exile.).

23 October
The radio stations *Balmaceda*[10] (in the hands of Christian Democrat financiers), *Agricultura* (controlled by the national organisation of large landowners (SNA), the main employers' corporation) and *Yungay* all seceded from the national network in concerted fashion within minutes of one another.

To celebrate these events, special programmes called *shows* were organised, with opposition senators and deputies appearing. On Radio Balmaceda the main attractions were an up-and-coming Christian Democrat deputy, the young leader of the Federation of School Students, as well as a Christian Democrat leader of the Central Trades Union Federation (CUT).

24 October
Large headline on the front page of *La Segunda* (popular evening daily published by the same group as *El Mercurio*) announces: "Sh . . . Homage by the Government to the day of silence: eleven radios closed down, three newspapers occupied, an illegal national network and journalists apprehended."

25 October
Two other opposition radios secede in turn and transmit. The show spreads to the streets where, to a soundtrack of pots and pans, elements of the extreme Right and the National Party organise a demonstration. Tyres burnt and barricades set up to celebrate "*Radio Mineria*, free radio".

28 October
Radio Chilena, the station of the Catholic church, secedes just in time: half an hour later, the President of the Republic puts an end to the national radio network.
   In all the provincial towns, similar events occurred.

Information and popular mobilisation

To appreciate the agitation tactics used by the opposition press during October, it is necessary to recall several past events. For the media had developed a constant awareness of the strategy of "mass resistance" adopted subsequently by the bourgeoisie when, after the success of the first big street demonstration – that of women in December 1971 – it realised that it did not have to depend on parliamentary methods. Within this option, the publishers distributed separate functions among themselves. But the campaign of agitation of mass fronts and, in parallel, of all more or less united groups which could be enrolled in the conspiracy of sedition, was only the culmination of a long-range strategy defined by the Right and expressed in its press.
   What was to undergo a radical change was the method of approaching audiences. As we have already pointed out, the most symptomatic change was that in the liberal concept of public opinion. The target of information ceased to be the passive consumer, the "average" individual of periods of "democratic" normality. The new target was defined in a precise and active way, in terms of the concrete place he or she occupied in the resistance and the specific interests motivating him or her. At least two lines of agitation can be pinpointed. One was addressed to a vast, disunited front: the consumer, the housewife, the taxpayer... goaded on with the repertory derived from the spectre of "Marxist totalitarianism" (the *goulag* had not yet been launched!). The other tended towards the more organic and was centred on the selective agitation of corporations, students, businesses and the professional associations (nurses, doctors, lawyers, architects, engineers, and so on).
   Thus, modifying its concept of public opinion in terms of the concrete political alliances it projected, the media inaugurated a

method of selecting, processing and distributing news in such a way as to reach more and more precise social categories. Several examples testify to this. During 1971 and 1972, *El Mercurio* devoted editorials every month to professional associations and transport and commerce corporations. In May 1971, for example, eight editorials were devoted to the problems of small tradesmen and truck owners. In August and September of the same year, there were seven and five editorials respectively; in December 1971 and January 1972, ten and eleven. As for professional associations, there were nine editorials on this theme in August 1971, a figure maintained during the year that followed. "Corporatist power" was evoked well before the October strike, as this editorial from *Mercurio* makes clear: "Today, we note a turning point: the individualism of the small farmer or the tradesman has been broken in the face of the urgent demand for solidarity." The goal of the press, radio and television stations was to work on these previously defined mass fronts.

A brief survey of the right-wing press during the twenty days preceding the "democratic march" on 10 October and the proclamation on an unlimited strike on the 11th shows three main axes around which the ideological offensive was organised:

1. The economic disaster.
2. The breakdown of social order.
3. The threats against freedom of expression.

The first theme was worked on from two perspectives: price increases, shortages and inflation on the one hand; the destruction of the economic system and the anarchy caused by nationalisation on the other. The first perspective was linked to the necessity to capitalise on the discontent of vast sectors of the population by playing on motivations of survival and consumption. The other worked more finely on specific fronts, fueling and channeling the anxiety of small- and medium-sized businesses (behind whom the industrial and monopolist sectors hid the defence of their own interests).

The alarmist content is clear from the following headlines in the days directly preceding the crisis. *La Prensa*: "The government has announced: no more veal or butter" (27 November); "We depend on the outside world not to die of hunger" (11 October). *El Mercurio*: "Galloping inflation would bring despair to households"; "The anguish of 99.8% (inflation): the crisis of the private economic sector;"[11] "Allende: we must adopt a war economy" (8 October). *La Segunda*: "Price increases are wiping out wage agreements" (3 October); "Private enterprise bankrupt: rationing soon" (7 October).

The spectre of hunger, pots and pans as the symbol of "civil resistance", the advance of Marxist totalitarianism leading to rationing cards, shortages as a foretaste of the socialist future, the cereal crisis in the USSR and the beans (the national food *par excellence*) that Chile was sending to Cuba, are just some of the innumerable arguments thrown together in this context.

The second axis related to the climate of violence and repression "set off by Popular Unity". The aim here was obviously to sow panic among the population, but the message was also directed at the armed forces and aimed at creating favourable conditions for a reactionary law on weapons control.[12] The news was full of references to "armed groups" associated with the government parties or the periphery of Popular Unity. These groups supposedly "provoked" the "democratic" forces, occupied schools, factories, marketplaces, and permanently outflanked the institutional forces of order. Let us emphasise a characteristic feature, however: the extension of the notion of extremism from outside the confines of paramilitary groups to encompass the embryo organisations of popular power. These included self-defence and surveillance committees, and the Supply and Price Control Committees (where working-class women were particularly active),[13] all of which were described as seditious groups. The image brandished in front of public opinion was that of a "Marxist government", a generator of violence, chaos and aggression against the individual and society. Aggression and Marxist repression legitimised, in return, a "democratic" defence.

The front page headlines were deliberately suggestive. *La Prensa*: "An armed commando of the Popular Unity at San-Borja hospital" (3 October); "Armed groups attempt to occupy the central market" (7 October); *El Mercurio*: "*Pobladores* (residents of the shanty towns and members of the Supply and Price Control Committees (JAP) attempt to take over the central market" (7 October); *La Segunda*: "On the order of the authorities, security guards break up a peaceful student march with truncheons, tear gas and water cannons" (3 October).

The third point is closely related to the others in its techniques. During these weeks, the campaign led by the bourgeoisie for the defence of press freedom intensified. This campaign was to serve as a framework for the meeting of the Inter-American Press Association (IAPA), which grouped newspaper owners from the two American hemispheres, and was held in Santiago during the first week of October. Furthermore, the calling of a "massive march for democracy" was in protest against the closure of *Radio Agricultura* (banned for forty-eight hours because it presented a simple street fight as a "confrontation between civilians and soldiers").

The meeting of all these powerful individuals led to a mobilisation and the calling of a "democratic demonstration" for 10 October. That day, *La Prensa* headlined: "No to hate, violence and hunger. Today, we shall march for liberty." Several hours later, *La Segunda* followed with: "Democracy protests today against the Marxist dictatorship, hate, sectarianism, hunger and inflation." These campaigns were also important in preparing the population for the later movement of employers' strikes, and giving them a spurious legality.

When the employers' strike broke out, right-wing journalism concentrated in monolithic fashion on propaganda for the movement. The victorious progression of the strike, the celebration of the total "paralysis" of the country, and the solidarity of the population with the corporatist movement, were the three principal themes of the journalistic "coverage" of the conflict. It was the perspective of the defence of "democratic principles" which assured its readability.

To project this triumphal image of the strike, the bourgeois press organised the facts unilaterally – its usual penchant, only exaggerated by the circumstances. In so doing it showed its purpose as simply to agitate one sector of the population and no longer to create a consensus between citizens, as in periods of normality. In effect, it overturned its relationship with reality. If it attained its publicity goal, it was precisely because it evaded or evacuated another side of the conflict: the response of the popular mobilisation, the voluntary work, the organisation of the "industrial belts", the formation of patriotic fronts which undermined the plan and overcame the consequences of the bourgeois insurrection.

Teletrece fulfilled a similar task to that of the press. Airtime had to be given to all the corporations supporting the strike, whose progression was promoted in minute detail. Any day, taken at random, is representative. On 17 October, seven interviews were presented, six in favour of the strike, one against. The latter was with a student leader from the Catholic University calling for a regrouping of "volunteers of the country". Fourteen minutes were assigned to the former, two minutes ten seconds to the latter. Some of the leaders interviewed were liable to arrest (and subsequently were), as *Teletrece* made clear. In spite of this, the journalists obtained their "scoop". Among those interviewed: the leader of the National Confederation of Owners of urban buses and collective taxis, the President of the National Federation of Taxi Drivers, the President of the National Confederation of Truck Owners (the notorious León Vilarin, the Chilean Jimmy Hoffa), the President of the Santiago section of the Doctors' Association...

The "people's" press

What catches one's attention in the operation of the press at this time is the appropriation of the concept of the "people", and its implied connotations, to characterise the contingents of strikers – mainly by attempting to reproduce within them a varied social spectrum. By virtue of the pluralist miracle of the press, the smiling young man from the residential quarter of Santiago shares a blanket with the old peasant from the south. In a more direct and spectacular manner, the photo sequences attempted to confirm day after day that the "democratic forces" – that is, the bosses – were supported by the majority. In this sum of mutually supporting individuals and wills, old people and children are prominent, although the preferential targets are women (and their instrument of struggle in the kitchen – the saucepan) and the small businessmen "workers", truckers and peasants. Prodigious paradox. Here, the newspaper which has historically accompanied the whole formation of bourgeois hegemony has become the extensive chronicler of the eternal down-and-outs.

An inventory of the civil resistance would be a long one: the town, the country, the solidarity of corporations and the people. At the centre, the "free communal soup" of the truckers: on any page, from any angle, tirelessly repeating the message of insurrection, an insurrection in the name of the "people".

The attributes of the corporatist leaders – moral integrity[17] and serenity – were also seen to respond to the sacrifice and courage of the strikers and their supporters. In the opposing camp, the Popular Unity supporters, whether those of the forces of order or civil contingents, were described as *creating* violence and aggression. When two citizens fought in the street, it was clear – but stressed in case there was any doubt – that the aggressor belonged to Popular Unity. The Right could not fail to offer proof of an important element in its cohesion: the repression of the forces of order against the bourgeois rabble (transformed in its version to the forces of order, manipulated by Popular Unity, against the people).

When one studies this initial impact as it appears in headlines, photos and layout, one sees the extent to which capitalising on the notion of "the people" is based on omission: there was no account of the working or peasant classes as a force organising its daily practice around the construction of a new order – a particularly tangible reality at the time. When reference was made to it, the proletariat appeared as the sum of disunited contingents preoccupied with trimming back "public liberties" and fired by violence. (Nothing had changed since the Commune!)

This mystification around the concept of "the people" was also the result of a task long refined by the bourgeois press with a view to requisitioning the political images of the Left and giving them a significance in line with its own ambitions. This tendency to capture, at the level of language, the conceptual arms of the workers and peasants' movement corresponded, in concrete political activity, to the appropriation of its methods of combat: the insurrectional strike, taken up by the bourgeoisie in October. But, as we have already remarked, at the same time that it achieved this appropriation of the methods of struggle of the working class, the bourgeoisie ensured its alibis, saving the institutional face. To legitimise itself, the corporatist strike placed itself within the framework of a legality imposed, but ridiculed, by a government accused of illegality. The government being characterised as the source of chaos, it was easy for the corporatist movement to present itself as the bastion of democratic principles.

The press campaign of the Right was at once united and diversified. In this relative diversity, it fell on *El Mercurio* systematically to take leading responsibility for the project of "corporatist power". A careful analysis of editorials produces significant results. Between 12 October and 5 November, *El Mercurio* devoted twenty-two editorials to corporations on strike, while celebrating the united front of sedition as a radically new historical phenomenon in the annals of national political life. These texts bring out the primary concern of projecting an image of the ecumenical nature of the interests protected by the bourgeois system. This "universal" image is based on the consensus that the bourgeoisie seeks to realise around the defence of private property. The plans for nationalisation served as an argument to extend its campaign into new areas of support for its strategy of overthrowing the popular government. And to accumulate support, it is necessary to define the points of convergence between the most diverse sectors.

Some examples:

"If the plunder suffered by large private economic interests has been unjust and illegal, the losses of small producers, who work with their own hands with the small amount of money they have succeeded in making during their existence, is much more dramatic..."
(Assault on the central market, 9 October, 1972)

"Corporatist solidarity is in the process of becoming the only effective weapon against the march of Popular Unity towards the absolute control of the means of subsistence of the country..."
(Significance of the transport strike, 12 October, 1972)

These examples enable us to see how the bourgeoisie justifies its power to represent majorities. The sequence of "plunder" as it is related by a bourgeois newspaper emphasises the progression – presented as the beginning of an irreversible future – of "totalitarian" control: "This began with the large – continued with the medium-sized and finally attacked the little." The texts secondly consolidate the image of an accumulation of diversified fronts, itemised throughout the social scale, by detaching the community from their interests. Finally, it emerges on to what became the axis of the October campaign: agitation around the "middle classes" by maintaining a constant progression towards the less well-off sectors in order to capitalise on their discontent and project the idea of "popular support".

It was in this populist vein that the employers sought daily to benefit at the height of the corporatist strike:

"The energetic opposition to the socialising [sic] offensive is more due to small businessmen, independent workers and modest landlords than to big business. The latter are content to demand compensation or be invited to participate in mixed economy companies. On the other hand, the owner who works with his hands and whose wealth is due only to his own effort lives concretely the values of liberty, property and democracy. He perceives the slightest threat to these values..."

(The Democratic Consensus, 15 October, 1972)

The "democratic consensus", which still served as a platform for the offensive on 15 October, broke up and crystallised into "corporatist power" a week later. At this stage of the crisis and the campaign of manipulation, the elementary categories of class used in previous editorials were dissolved. To fabricate its class cohesion, the bourgeoisie needed to eliminate the slightest suspicion of difference between the interests of the sectors on strike. So the movement which began in terms of the defence of private property led on to the constitution of a front which, although diversified from a professional point of view, was nevertheless homogeneous and monolithic.

"Popular Unity has wanted to see this strike as a strike of the bourgeoisie. Now those who have participated in the strike include truckers, small shopkeepers, artisans and small businessmen, workers, peasants, technicians and professionals among others. The social composition of the corporations on strike cannot be qualified as bourgeois, working class or peasant. Various social conditions have come together in this movement because it is the activity or particular position of the individual which is more important, and not an artificial classification in terms of the opposition of exploiters/exploited."

(Corporatist Power, 22 October, 1972)

During the October crisis, as we can see in these extracts, the bourgeoisie's attempted annexation of numerous social sectors reached its peak. The task of the right-wing press was to display widespread popular support, for want of which the bourgeoisie cannot "democratically" legitimise its historical plan and in particular the tactics used to destabilise authority and the legitimacy of a popular government. For this, the press created its own "popular front", an active contingent in a period of mounting crisis, a reserve army in a time of ebb. While the battle of the bourgeoisie reached its conclusion and its battalions returned to their winter quarters to prepare themselves for the next skirmish – electoral this time[15] – corporatist power underwent, at the level of journalistic language, its final transformation.

Located, evaluated in their real colours, the people of the bourgeoisie now had a name:

"Some partisans of the Popular Unity think that it is a strike of the bourgeoisie, business executives, bosses. Faithful to their Marxist position, they still dream of the world of English capitalism last century, that known by their master thinker: a few rich exploiters and a multitude of exploited paupers. This does not correspond to reality in Chile today. For years, we have been practising among ourselves an energetic redistribution of income. The traditional upper class merges into the middle bourgeoisie, many workers belong to the bourgeois class and even the peasants from co-operatives are tending to become bourgeois.

"The middle classes reflect the majority of the country because our democracy is truly egalitarian. The corporatist strike expresses the 'no' of the middle classes which is the 'no' of the majority..."

(The majority protests, 29 October, 1972)

This "people" from the middle classes was to shatter dramatically on the morning after the coup. The only valid negotiators recognised by the junta were the employers' corporations.

2: The feminine side of the coup
of the coup

"When we saw the women of Chile on the march, we knew that Allende's days were numbered." A Brazilian engineer (who acknowledged other interests than those of his profession) talking to a journalist from the *Washington Post* in January, 1974.[1] During the same interview he claimed that direct responsibility for mobilising the women belonged to far-right-wing organisations and Brazilian bosses. "We taught the Chileans to use their women against the Marxists." Of course, this arrogance and assurance is displayed only now, when sedition has apparently been crowned with success. But this spokesman for the Brazilian reactionaries is not a man to overlook the possible implications of this type of experience. And by now the active rôle of women in counter-insurgency is practically a doctrine in the field, though he seems to discover it for the first time:

"Women are the most effective political weapon . . . They have time; they are endowed with a great emotional capacity and they mobilise very rapidly. If one wishes, for example, to spread the rumour that the President is inclined to drink, or that he has health problems, just use women. By the next day the story will be all over the country . . . The usefulness of women lies in the fact that they can convince the military that they are supported by an important sector of the population."

The last sentence shows us that, according to the logic of sedition, mass demonstrations of the Right – particularly those expressing women's opposition – are no more than new forms of old campaigns designed to stir up public opinion towards one final objective: to set the military side of the plot into motion. "They begged us for three years," said Pinochet the day after the coup, offering thanks to the "democratic" mass media and emphasising the effectiveness of women's constant pleas. The Brazilian engineer, moreover, traced the line of continuity between women's demonstrations and rumour and public opinion campaigns. He revealed that Brazil, in addition to lending paramilitary support, aided the Chilean Right in two ways: planning for the mobilization of women, and creating public opinion research centres. For the Right's ideological battle against the popular regime, carried out for the "conquest of souls" to use its own expression, was not only implemented through propaganda leaflets. It came to life in the streets. It no longer relied solely on a few minds capable of turning out propaganda. The whole counter-revolutionary potential of its female constituency, converted into an army of mass activists, was thrown into the fray. Women served as a "democratic" front for the brutal coup in the same way as professional and employers' associations had done.

And, in speeches, women were used to goad men's consciences. For example:

"The women really taught us, the men, a lesson. They never lowered their heads by accepting something they did not want; they proved themselves unyielding, ready to defend what was just. They met every challenge with resistance. We want them to participate in the administration of this country. The women will play as important a rôle as the trade associations, the armed forces and the political parties."[2]

General Leigh spoke these words – an unusual postscript to the annals of world fascism – in the days immediately following the coup. As a sign of gratitude for her services, the Chilean woman was to be rewarded with direct representation in the future "Parliament", alongside corporations, the Armed Forces and youth. Today, in the Junta's more recent declarations, there is more caution, and even a reluctance, to bring up this issue,[3] though the generals, who increasingly postpone handing over power to their civilian accomplices in the coup, have not discarded "feminist" proclamations, in which they emphasise that women are one of the pillars of "national reconstruction".

Nevertheless, an important question remains to be answered: what happened to the conception of women in the dominant ideology? It is necessary to appraise the full importance of this question accurately, because the traditional image of women, nurtured by the Chilean bourgeoisie (as much or more than any other bourgeoisie), was at the point of breaking down. On the one hand, all the essential characteristics consecrated by the dominant ideology in order to build and reproduce the "feminine" order were, in effect, present: respect for private property, non-participation in politics, the so-called feminine inclination to see and understand everything, and confinement to discriminatory interests and tasks. On the other hand, and in violent contrast, the bourgeoisie overnight proposed that its women adopt those aspects of themselves which constituted "another" feminine reality: women in politics, women in the violent streets, streets which were no longer for window-shopping. They created a mass-produced "Pasionaria" who leads men into combat, is not content simply to wait for the soldiers – her sons, husband or father – to return from war, but who is by no means a singular heroine, in the style of Inez de Suárez, lover of the *conquistador* Pedro de Valdivia, who singlehandedly defended the fort of Santiago against the "savages". Not a heroine because, in the end, these unique women only serve to consecrate the normality of a life outside of combats. By examining the ideological mechanisms used by the Chilean Right, we can avoid the misconception that the Right's mass-mobilisation of its feminine contingent could lead to a decisive breakdown of the traditional image of women.

The three years of popular rule in Chile enable us to expose in

action the profoundly anti-liberationist basis of a women's movement for political emancipation promoted by a bourgeoisie which
saw its class interests threatened. At the same time that the Chilean
experience reveals the elasticity of the bourgeois concept of
"femininity", it also shows the limitations of "liberation" movements based on these concepts. Furthermore, Chile provides us with
a *model for the exploitation of women*, at both the political and
ideological levels, that can be applied not only to other Latin
American countries, but also to the metropolitan countries where
leftist forces may be presented with the possibility of reaching
government by virtue of the rules of the democratic game.

It is certainly important to emphasise the particular characteristics of the Chilean case, and likewise the unique aspects of the
situation of Chilean women. But we must not forget or lose sight of
the fact that reactionaries everywhere, through instinct or the will to
survive, are capable of generating an ominous universalisation of
their methods and strategies. There are already quite enough
examples to confirm this.

A number of episodes attest to the constant presence of women in
the crucial moments of class confrontation during the three years of
the popular regime. These episodes enable us to define the social
composition of the female population that was opposed to Salvador
Allende. We will cite them as they come to mind.

Allende was elected with 36.2 per cent of the vote on 4 September,
1970. The majority of the female electorate preferred the candidates
of the Right: 68.3 per cent of the women voted either for Alessandri of
the National Party (38.4 per cent) or Tomic of Christian Democracy
(29.9 per cent), while Allende won only 30.5 per cent of the women's
vote.[4]

During the period between the elections and the date when the
popular forces took office, a group of the oligarchy's women dressed
completely in black, like birds of ill-fortune, surrounded the Moneda
in a funeral procession, mourning "the disappearance of democracy
in Chile".

A year and a half later another woman from the oligarchy
stationed her horse in front of the same palace, protesting the
threatened expropriation of her large landholding. She had travelled
by horseback the long distance between the capital and her farm in
the south, gathering support from the constituency of right-wing
parties along the way. The conservative press hailed her as the
Amazon of Liberty. One grotesque detail remains to be mentioned.
Dressed in a bathing suit, she paraded on horseback through the
streets of Santiago, no doubt to symbolise – assuming we want to read
any dignity at all into this spectacle – the state of deprivation to which

Popular Unity had reduced her.

The Right's first mass demonstration was carried out by women. The last one before the coup was also a woman's demonstration. That famous first protest, the "March of the Empty Pots and Pans" which took place in December, 1971, was one of the factors which led Fidel Castro, then visiting Chile, to declare in his last speech in the National Stadium: "During this first year, the reactionaries have learned more, and more quickly, than the revolutionaries." Organised by the Democratic Women's Front, which joined together the female supporters of the National and Christian Democratic parties, this demonstration was the first opportunity for the Right, still hesitant and indecisive about which strategy to adopt, to measure the effectiveness of these street actions. In March 1972, the Right decided to rely primarily upon its "masses", relegating to a secondary position traditional means of pressure and attack (the parliament, the courts, the parties, the Comptroller's office – a kind of auditor's office converted into a veritable state within the state). The demonstrations were repeated regularly. In all of them the symbol and noisemaker was an empty pot beaten with its top or with a cooking spoon. After that famous night of 1 December, the echo of pots resounded in all the residential neighbourhoods of all Chilean cities. The "tam-tam" of the empty pots was to the Right what the "yu-yu" was to the women of the liberation forces of Algeria. Two weeks could not pass without the metallic meeting-call being sounded on the street corners, between eight and ten at night.

The women's demonstrations were always carried out in the same way. The main contingent was made up of bourgeois women of all ages who arrived in automobiles, often accompanied by their maids; next a considerable number of *petit-bourgeois* women and, finally, a minority of women from the poorer districts (and shanty-towns) and the lumpen. All were encircled by helmeted, chain-bearing militants of the extreme Right's paramilitary group, "Fatherland and Liberty", which had an active women's branch and was openly seditious. Not until the last months of the popular regime, however, did Women's Power (see previous section) come to control the women's front.

We come upon the bourgeois women once again when the opposition parties openly began to woo the Armed Forces. On several occasions these women were responsible for provoking the Army, stirring up the soldiers' machismo and ambitions of power. As a sign of reproach for what they considered a lack of virility in the Chilean soldiers, these women often threw corn at the walls of the Military Academy, as one throws feed to barnyard chickens! When Popular Unity tried to resolve the problem of scarcity of products by creating the JAPs (distribution and price control committees) right-wing women supported the merchants' opposition to this egalitarian distribution system, sabotaging the JAPs (with greater or lesser success, depending on the neighbourhood). They launched the same kind of open aggression on policemen stationed at the JAP locations, raining insults, jeers, even coins upon them, to leave no doubt about their contempt for those who had "sold out" to the popular government.

While women mobilised by the Right were banging empty pots, many working-class and poor women were mobilising to demand nationalisation of all private food distribution. These women were particularly active in the people's markets that were set up to distribute the food controlled by the state sector (twenty-eight per cent of the total) and in the campaign to increase state control of that sector. Right-wing propaganda, on the other hand, made much of the food shortages that they themselves had helped to induce through massive hoarding, the famous truckers' strike of October 1972, bosses lock-outs and active sabotage of the people's markets. As well, beyond the limits of the community, women actively participated along with men in the struggles of the Left. Finally, recall the harassment inflicted by an upper-class woman on General Prats, who was accused of holding the Army to its constitutionalist heritage. On 27 June, 1973, two days before an abortive coup, "Fatherland and Liberty" sent one of its women to harass General Prats, Minister of the Interior and Commander-in-Chief of the Army, as he was being driven to work. She followed his car, repeatedly shouting insults at him. This led to a major incident when she later charged that Prats took out his gun and fired at her car.

That individual protest took place on a collective dimension after the frustrated coup of 29 June, 1973, when groups of officers' wives (the same ones who offered their jewels and wedding rings to the Junta to save the Treasury and begin the process of "national reconstruction") demonstrated under General Prats' window to make his position more intolerable and thereby erode his moral strength. The Brazilian engineer mentioned earlier pointed out the daily influence that a woman can exert on those around her, noting that the military, like everyone, have wives and homes, and are not free from that influence.

The corrosive force of the women's demonstrations finally erupted eight days before the coup of 11 September, on the occasion of the biggest march organised by the Chilean Right. During the march, the women shouted slogans demanding Allende's resignation. Later, the Brazilians who helped organise the march compared it to the women's protest in Sao Paulo which preceded the fall of Joao Goulart in 1964. It should be noted, however, to limit the application of this comparison, that, contrary to Brazil, where the demonstrators marched while reciting their rosaries, the Chilean Right did not so often appeal to its women's sense of religion (a slightly shaky tactic as far as the Chilean urban masses are concerned). One exception to this occurred. Religious sympathies were brought into play during the period when the great theme of mobilisation against the popular regime was the planned teaching reform – the National Unified School (ENU) Project. In this dispute, the clerical tendency took sides in the classic antagonism between public and private schools. However, once the coup occurred, the clerical tendency took on the position of an invading force, attempting to restore order to the Chilean home by assigning to everyone, particularly women, the place traditionally allotted them.

The opposition women's movement was not limited to sectors of the upper and middle bourgeoisie, as the above examples tend to indicate. The Right also had the support of certain working-class and *petit-bourgeois* women. There were two ways in which these women could participate. Firstly, they worked with community organisations created by the previous government and in many cases still controlled by Christian Democrats. Among these organisations were the *centros de madres* (women's centres – a type of workshop set up in the poorer neighbourhoods) and the *juntas de vecinos* (neighbourhood boards for the administration of local matters, composed of both men and women and strongly influenced by the women). While the Christian Democrats still appeared to be the main opposition force (until October, 1972) the Right organised several demonstrations of *pobladoras* (inhabitants of the shanty-towns). The other way in which working-class and *petit-bourgeois* women participated was in demonstrations in support of the strike movement involving their husbands, sons and brothers. The wives of the strikers at El Teniente copper mine were called "the heroic wives of the miners" by the right-wing press, which was delighted to be able to claim a women's solidarity movement of the kind which had previously belonged exclusively to the leftist tradition of struggle for the emancipation of the Latin American people (for example, the marches organised by the miners' wives in Bolivia).[5] The truckers' wives prepared "free communal soup" on the street corners of Santiago to attract the pity of passers-by and to gain the general public's support. At the same time, their husbands received far more than they could have earned by working, in return for carrying on their strike. When the coup broke out, it was the truckers' wives who were found on the stairs of the Senate in the midst of a hunger strike already several days old.

One of the rallying calls to what was to be the last demonstration lists all the sections of the female population that the opposition claimed to represent. It also indicates the level of hysteria attained by the subversive movement.

> Chilean women:
> Mr Allende does not deserve to be President of the Republic.
> Mr Allende has led this country to catastrophe.
> We have no bread for our children!
> We have no medicine for our sick!
> We have no clothes to keep ourselves warm!
> We have no walls for shelter!
> We have been harassed and persecuted for defending our sons, for supporting our striking husbands, for taking to the streets to stir up the sleeping consciousness of so many people.
> We call all women to a commitment of honour!
> Wednesday, September 5, at 5.00 pm.
> We call on women transport workers, women of the *Papelera*, peasant women, *pobladoras*, women students and merchants, secretaries, nurses, social workers, housewives, professional women and women of Chile's *Gremios*.[6]

Note the proletarian ring to the demands of the bourgeois woman! In effect, a movement of double mystification was in operation. Even though women of diverse social sectors co-existed in the ranks of the Right, they did so in widely differing proportions, a fact which these invitations had no interest in revealing. By putting a few women from the popular classes in the front lines, the bourgeoisie waved the flags of the proletariat. Its collective action usurped the banners of the poor, for whom the price of bread is always what matters most. (Of course, the popular government was doing everything possible to protect the price and supply of bread.) Consumption – that necessary ritual of the bourgeois woman – usually directed towards luxury goods, was presented as an issue of survival based on the needs of bare subsistence.

Yet there are limits to this so-called solidarity. One should not think that the women of the Right, in the vast majority members of the moneyed class, abandoned their class stereotypes or divested themselves of their sense of superiority when they moved a step closer to the women of other classes. The only change produced by the war-time conditions was that they only manifested their haughtiness explicitly when they confronted poorer women who refused to join the ranks of bourgeois women. Then the abusive tongues were quick to harp on the distance between "social positions", a distance to be overcome only within the limits set by the bourgeoisie. "Look at those plebeians! Who do they think they are?" exclaimed the bourgeois women when they saw the women of the revolutionary masses (their sisters!) trying to organise food distribution systems in their communities by themselves.

That was the showy side of the women's opposition to the Popular Unity government. But this opposition also had an everyday side, the incessant traffic in rumours carried out in the home or among groups of friends in the neighbourhoods. If the principal attack dealt with a lack of food, the principal focus was hoarding. Both points proceed from the same definition of the woman. She runs out into the street to demand bread, while she implacably builds up her storehouse. This is described in a song which was sung so many times during popular demonstrations: "The right has two pots, one very small and one quite large/The first is beaten in the streets, the second is used to hoard and accumulate...".[7]

"There's no meat, there're no eggs/In this new Chile," shouted the women of the Right in front of the Moneda, while daily, like seditious ants, they participated in the wilful destruction of the national economy by amassing stockpiles (whose size varied with social status, since "hardships" had failed to bring about the miracle of levelling differences in incomes!) and organising and feeding the black market. Acting on the basis of that imaginary community of interests which supposedly unites housewives of all social classes, this household opposition constituted the everyday side of the demonstrations which periodically invaded the streets.

Another powerful issue was the defence of children from the "Marxist yoke". This issue was brought up more sporadically, usually through the *centros de apoderados* (parent-teacher associations) which were organised in national federations and relied on the decisive support of ruling-class and *petit-bourgeois* mothers.

The pages of *El Mercurio*, the oldest newspaper of the Chilean bourgeoisie, were filled with evidence that the Right was not about to exclude women, and the organisations in which they were present, from a strategy to overthrow the popular government, particularly when this strategy rested on the mobilisation of mass movements. Women's new civic duties are quite clearly defined in those pages:

"No housewife, no neighbour, no person who is presently capable of action or expression, has any right to wait for others to defend the freedom of this country. Community, school, workplace and other organisations ought to receive the support of these democratic masses."

While the bourgeoisie waited until 1949 to reluctantly grant women the right to vote (a right which they had demanded since 1898) and never favoured their petitions for civil rights, under war-time conditions they suddenly rushed to open a loophole in their implicit codes. They could no longer be openly content with the fact that women were given passive roles – as mothers, spouses, housewives – through which they had traditionally guaranteed the reproduction of society's crucial values. It was necessary for women to become active, organising and mobilising themselves to defend "democracy", becoming in the process its living symbol as woman-spouse, woman-housewife, woman-Homeland. Paradoxically, the particular element which the Right was counting on, and which it used with impunity, arose precisely from a sacred part of the dominant ideology – the division between women and politics. This separation, once unconsciously present in every individual (as is the case with all collective symbols) allowed the bourgeoisie to present the woman's new activity as devoid of political content and to have it accepted as such. Traditional symbols and values which unequivocally defined the meaning of women's behaviour were relied upon to legitimise these demonstrations. Demonstrations were seen as the spontaneous reaction of the most apolitical sector of public opinion, brought together and activated by a natural survival instinct. This so-called "democratic" sector "naturally" sought to defend the traditions and values of "justice" and "liberty" which mask the oppressive course of bourgeois order.

The words used in another invitation to the last right-wing demonstration show how the bourgeoisie claimed to represent the working people by means of the woman-mother symbol (i.e., the woman as reproducer of labour power). The wording also shows how, bolstered by this sudden "popular" majority created by sleight of hand, the bourgeoisie painted its most violent rallying cries to counter-revolution in democratic colours.

Chilean women:
Mr Allende says he will submit his resignation if the working people request it.
We are the people! Every child of this land was born from us!
Today, Wednesday the 5th, at 5 pm, in front of the Catholic University and in every Chilean city, women will make Mr Allende fulfil his promise.
No woman can fail to be present today at 5 pm.[8]

The bourgeoisie was able to hide its class interests behind the protests of mothers and housewives, behind demands which appeared unrelated to class strategy because they encompassed areas traditionally marginalised from the political sphere, such as the home, family organisation, rearing and education of children. On the other hand, within the repertoire of demands which emerged from these demonstrations, the Right tried – its caution diminishing more each time – to move beyond the specific field of women to surreptitiously include clearly political demands shared with other opposition sections.

The particular importance of these activities to the bourgeoisie and the ideological and political benefits which they extracted from them were made clear in the conservative press accounts of demonstrations like the march of the "empty pots". Did they not, in fact, help the bourgeoisie legitimise, "naturalise" – we could almost say "sanctify" – their seditious plan against the popular regime? In the chronology of violence published by *El Mercurio* (1st June, 1972) under the heading "1971–72: A Year of Violence Under Popular Unity," we read:

"December 1: the largest demonstration of women in the country's history ended in criminal aggression against the women by brigades of Popular Unity counter-demonstrators . . . 'The march of the empty pots' was intercepted by police only a few yards from the intersection of the Alameda and Miraflores Street where *carabineros* threw tear gas bombs, causing the indignation of the marching women and spectators."

The marchers themselves denounced this treatment, and the following day the same newspaper carried the sensationalist headline: "Although We Were Women, They Beat Us!" Women threw themselves body and soul into this new activity which, for many, replaced the sacrosanct Wednesday or Thursday "tea parties" (*te canasta*). "Of course, darling, go out and demonstrate!"

The purpose of these accounts and commentaries is to convey the image of a Marxist government as the instigator of violence, chaos and aggression against women and the community. The loss of the code of gallantry, although women were the first to break it, was hailed as the first sign of the total destruction of civilisation obstinately sought by Allende. "Democratic" defence was the authorised response to supposed Marxist aggression and repression.

This same symbolic point appears – this time even further embellished – in *El Mercurio*'s account of another incident, published in the same chronology of violence.

"March 22: a demonstration by a group of cripples against the legal red-tape required to import artificial limbs and other implements, turned into a heated confrontation with *carabineros* who carried out the orders of their superiors with excessive force."

Weakness... Innocence... Defencelessness... (Women cripples.) Lacking a "responsible" father, the bourgeoisie granted itself the right to represent and defend all the meek and oppressed of God's earth.

They revived all the stereotypes of femininity (sweetness, sensitivity, a natural inclination to peace and order) in order to cover their seditious movement with a veil of innocence and to imply or reinforce the idea that the system that women approved of and would defend when "compelled" by circumstances, was the appropriate system for the country, the system sought by all respectable Chileans. The other way, on the other hand, was full of deception. The people who supported it were few in number and were only captives of violence and fanaticism.

The constitution promised by the military Junta the day after the coup was to guarantee representation to women in "Parliament", along with corporations, the Armed Forces, youth and political parties. Throughout their entire period of opposition to the popular regime, the bourgeoisie cultivated this notion of the *natural* corporatism of women, a conception which was implicit in the presentation of the women's movement as a democratic movement. At first, the women's front, coupled with such issues as the shortage of supplies, allowed the Right to mobilise women and, through them, the *consumer* (that anonymous representative of the middle class), against the policies of Popular Unity. But a mixture of ideas based on a corporatist ideology was already implicit in the creation of this front. This took shape in the course of the struggle and crystallised as a conceptual and practical response to Marxism, proposing to rebuild society on the basis of corporatist power.[9]

By defining women on the basis of *natural* rather than historical attributes, the dominant ideology laid the groundwork for the conception of women's corporatism which emerged from the Junta's declaration. The concept of women which cloaked the ruling class ideology was used, in effect, to avoid class antagonisms and to obscure the understanding that class, not individual contradictions were primary. Thanks to the universal character of Nature, the condition of being a woman would guarantee the fundamental unity of interests between all women, over and beyond any social, economic or ideological differences. This conception of women (which gained a formidable tactical rationality in the struggle) provided a tangible bond which cut through all social classes. "Women's Power" protected itself with the same democratic façade as corporativist power which brings together and joins individuals according to their "speciality". There is a feminine specialisation and function, just as there is a specialisation to all official groups.

Worried that, in the long run, women might acquire bad habits in the streets, such as the taste for political power, the bourgeoisie was even more eager to lock their women into clearly defined specialities and functions. We cannot fail to notice a similarity to the fate of business corporations, which were goaded to open political action during the entire counter-revolutionary phase and then restricted to their purely technical functions by the Right once it had regained state power. The same procedure was applied to women, who were told to return to their kitchens. Listen to Mrs Pinochet piously admonishing her counterparts while the Moneda Palace still smouldered and the Mapocho River carried away the first corpses:

"The cry from your hearts will be the salvation of everyone.

"Mothers, do not allow the children whom you put to sleep or comfort with tenderness and sacrifice to be struck by hate, that evil which turns human beings into beasts who destroy their fellow creatures... She who is speaking to you is but another mother who knows you can do much for peace and understanding among Chileans."[10]

Listen to the leaders of "Women's Power":

"Chilean women, whose suffering, humiliation and heroism saved the hope of freedom for Chile... know that Chile's reconstruction will be a task worthy of a disciplined and patriotic people. Therefore, *Women's Power* calls upon all Chilean women to demonstrate once again their inexhaustible spirit of sacrifice."[11]

Self-denial. Spirit of sacrifice. Love. How distant are the hate and maliciousness aimed at Allende before the bullets struck him down!

"Women's Power" seems to be nothing more than women's natural disposition towards passivity. The traditional image of women, which the Junta's rhetoric glorified in its full reactionary sense, emerged safe and sound from this confrontation with history to restore women to their pedestal as titular guardians of Family, Homeland and Property. It is not by chance that these three words, these three principles, were precisely those of *Fatherland and Liberty*'s programme, which today gives guidance to the *putschist* generals.

We will highlight three of the many factors which help to explain how the Chilean Right was able to mobilise this important and effective woman's front when it wanted: 1) the presence – both mythical and real – of certain features in the personality of Chilean women; 2) the existence of earlier mechanisms for the participation and organisation of women; and 3) the characteristics of women's integration into the production process.

"Tell me, Cazota, is everything in your country as beautiful as its women? In that case I congratulate you." These words of Louis Philippe to the new Chilean Ambassador to France were reported by a chronicler at the beginning of the century.[12] He went on to say: "Throughout this country's history, women have held a position of honour in society, whatever the means by which they exercised the loving influence of their superior spirit." These words, which could have been spoken by a contemporary, go beyond the tourist's myth that in Chile, the beauty of women is only equalled by the warmth and body of the wine.

Political crises typically reveal certain features in society not part of the upheaval itself. The convulsive developments in the actions of these Chilean women over the last three years was due, in great part, to the particular conditions of women in this country. While ruling class culture has integrated the values which sanctify the subordinate status of women (as in all capitalist societies), in practice women play a central rôle in the economics and organisation of the family. So much so, in fact, that some have claimed a matriarchy exists in Chile. This situation is particularly clear in the proletariat. Common law marriages are frequent, and as the men often abandon the home, women become the real pillar of family unity and act in an appropriate fashion. In recognition of this, the popular government passed a bill which granted unmarried women family allowances. Among the well-to-do sectors, in addition to exercising an indisputable authority in the home with the help of one or more maids,[13] women also were active in the public domain, though this was always within the discriminatory, if little disputed, framework of what was considered a woman's work: social services, teaching, interior decorating, secretarial work or paramedical services.[14]

Although, strictly speaking, there was no feminist movement in Chile, a small group of women from the ruling class distinguished itself in the early decades of the century in the struggles it waged for political and civil rights. At that time the women did not take to the streets, but, on 8 January, 1948, about forty women burst into the Chamber of Deputies and forced the men of their own class to grant them the right to vote. However, the leaders of the women's movement against the popular regime seemed to be successors of what was previously called "The Ladies' Club" rather than this handful of young suffragettes or the Women's Civic Party. The Women's Civic Party, organised at the same time as the Student Federation in 1920, fought for the right to vote but then lost all popular support when it campaigned to legalise divorce. The "Ladies' Club", made up of the most upper-crust aristocrats, clamoured against such scandalous behaviour and, by calling it a threat to good manners and family stability, managed to have the party dissolved. The short-lived Movement for Women's Emancipation, which followed, was attacked for its "communist tendencies", although it was not linked to any leftist ideology.

It was not until 1970 that the participation of women from the bourgeoisie ceased to revolve around a few individuals and took on real significance. At that time, "concern for their homes and families made them leave the tranquillity of the household and awakened in them the instincts of a she-wolf who saw her offspring attacked by the Popular Unity government." And, "by the historic 'March of the Empty Pots and Pans', they showed the government that – if necessary, they would leave their cosy kitchens to go on the warpath."[15] Until that time, however great their energetic and strong temperaments, and however much they appeared to seek independence and "liberation", these ruling-class Chilean women had always acted along lines prescribed by male authorities. No doubt they thought the "light" burden of their servitude was a thousand times compensated for by the advantages they gained: order and comfort inside their homes, relative freedom of movement outside the household and the "veneration" of the "stronger sex". Their activities only served to reveal the high price they attached to this order.

The formation of a women's "popular front" was no doubt facilitated by the mechanisms of women's integration instituted by the previous administration. The Right was finally able to capitalise on the "social integration" of the population which the "participation-oriented" Frei administration had encouraged. They set up a network of organisations at grassroots level, such as neighbourhood committees, cultural centres and, above all, women's centres (*centros de madres*). We should point out, however, that the women's centres, as well as other grass-roots organisations, were to become battlegrounds between the Right and the Left. More than once, the struggles which were fought there favoured the progressive forces. For example, it was due to the co-operation of many of the women's centres that the supply and price control committees (JAPs), of which we spoke earlier, were able to function in the poorer neighbourhoods.[16] Generally speaking, however, these community level organisations, particularly within the poorer communities, were organised according to the principles of aid to "marginalised" people. In other words, they were based on norms of participation and ideological frameworks which, given a climate of constant confrontation and the assistance of right-wing parties, made them effective tools in the mobilisation of women in favour of the traditional system. These women's centres brought together a group of mothers to carry out specifically women-orientated tasks. These women increasingly confirmed themselves in and limited themselves to their exclusive rôle as mothers and wives under the tutelage of women from the middle and even upper bourgeoisie. In exchange for their services, the bourgeois women gained electoral support for their candidates. Conceived to integrate "ordinary" women into a "communitarian" society, these centres reinforced a conservative ideology. Under the façade of "participation", they drew women away from any political action or affiliation which went against the system. They created the illusion of neutralising or overcoming the effects of marginalisation felt by poorer women, thereby diffusing the explosiveness of the situation. Learning once again to be obedient, many working-class women were effectively immobilised.

Furthermore, these centres developed norms and habits of co-existence between bourgeois and proletarian women, cultivating the traditional relationship with the *patrona*. This relationship was directly tied to a phenomenon which grew considerably under the popular government. When the food supply problem became a daily concern, it was not uncommon for working-class women to wait in long lines at the market place to purchase goods at the official price and then sell them at a good price (although not as high as the black market price) to *madrinas* (patrons) in the wealthier neighbourhoods.

Therefore, when we consider the characteristics of women's participation in the process of production, we realise that working-class Chilean women and particularly from the *petit bourgeoisie*, are most affected by the mechanisms of socialisation and participation which exist at the community level. In fact, the vast majority of the female population remains outside the process of economic production. According to the 1970 census, only slightly more than nineteen per cent of women above the age of twelve earn wages for work outside the home, compared with sixty-nine per cent of men. In terms of the adult family, that figure falls to eleven per cent for women. Many women withdraw from paid labour because of marriage and family duties and, contrary to what occurs in more developed countries, they do not reintegrate themselves into the work force at a later date. Moreover, the employment sectors which they enter, because of tradition and a lack of real choice, further reduce the possibilities of their being exposed to a different orientation than that prevailing in the above described organisations. Almost forty per cent of working women are employed as servants or do washing or ironing in private homes, a kind of work which tends to break down the bonds of solidarity with their own class. An indication of the extent of their exploitation is the fact that less than forty-five per cent of these women are registered by their employer for social security benefits. Twenty per cent of economically active Chilean women are factory workers, of which a very small percentage are unionised. The remainder is divided among professionals and skilled workers (sixteen per cent) and employees of the state or private enterprise (twenty-five per cent) as secretaries, saleswomen, etc. The meagre professional qualifications of *petit-bourgeois* women and their resultant fear of change make them even more vulnerable to the Right's blackmail.[17] If this were not the case, the reactionary professional associations would not have bothered to incorporate them but would have used them simply in their capacity as housewives.

In fact, the few professional associations (*colegios*) in which women were in the majority fully participated in the Central Confederation of Chilean Professional Associations (*Confederación Unica de las Corporaciones Profesionales de Chile*). Founded in 1971, it became the first corporatist front against Popular Unity. Among the participants were the Nurses' Association, the Social Workers' Association, the Midwives' Association, the Librarians' Association.

It is clear that all the factors which contributed to and explain the formation of a right-wing women's movement resulted from one important determinant: the relationship between women and the state in a capitalist society. In the period of intensifying class struggle which Chile experienced between 1970 and 1973, women who were dependent on, and complicit in, bourgeois ideology reproduced in the face of what they mistakenly understood to be an institutional crisis the same behaviour as that prescribed by the dominant culture in terms of their relations to men. In times of peace, the ruling class tries to avoid identifying the power of the state with the power of men, so as to leave women with the illusion that they, just like *every* citizen, are equal before the law, and can maintain a democratic relationship with the state. However, when the state changes hands and bourgeois control is threatened, women who are under the influence of a daily reinforced bourgeois ideology tend to resent the conflict, seeing it as a desertion of "virile elements" from the institutions which usually protect them. In order to struggle against a usurping "Marxist authority" (synonymous with chaos), they appealed to the principles of respect for authority (synonymous with order). Take, for example, the case of the women who threw corn at soldiers as if they were chickens. This was a clear-cut example of the fact that to these militant women supporters of the bourgeois order, control of the state was an affair for males and guaranteed their legitimate authority over women. This state, represented by the forces of order, had to symbolise a macho among machos. The women were no longer afraid to transgress their "code of feminine discretion and modesty".

Macho semantics appear throughout the favourite list of insults which the women used against the popular masses and against the forces of order which remained loyal to the government. The constitutionalist soldiers and the merchants who co-operated with the JAPs were called "cowards", "homosexuals", "sodomists". All of this meant: "you can't get it up" or, in other words, "you're impotent."

The most advanced sectors of the working class had a clear understanding of the rôle which the bourgeois media would play when the bourgeoisie went on the offensive. The following observations by two Santiago factory workers[18] indicate that they had accurately assessed women's particular vulnerability to this strategy of journalistic manipulation. Moreover, they reveal why women respond differently from men.

"Through the news, the headlines of their newspapers or radio programmes, the reactionaries everywhere gave preferential treatment to women. The latter, who do not always understand what is going on, believe these lies and begin to talk against the government.

"It does not affect us men as much because *we* do not listen to the radio all day; this cannot happen in the factory because we hold meetings, there is a higher level of consciousness and they cannot deceive us. But when we come home we are faced with something else and sometimes you cannot convince them."

We often forget that women's confinement to the home is the constant reference point for television and radio programming. This is particularly true for the radio, which literally follows working-class women around in their domestic work, making their "exile" sweeter and more gratifying, reproducing and highlighting the conditions which led to their defeated state. How many hours of radio and television programming, soap operas and radio serials, have as their primary objective the production and satisfaction of demands which grow out of a woman's own sense of alienation! While true in times of peace, this is doubly true in times of war when direct calls to action and the slow distillation of psychosis replace melodrama and lukewarm sentimentality.

To understand the full meaning of this phenomenon, we must consider not only the qualitative rupture between the newspapers that supported the popular government and the media controlled by the Right, but also have to take into account the purely quantitative aspect. The bourgeoisie not only retained its communications apparatus intact. It even expanded it, creating magazines and newspapers like *Tribuna*, which daily spat out headlines insulting the president. The bourgeoisie lost some of its power only in the area of television because the state network (the only national network) was automatically controlled by the new government. The government, however, had to allow pluralistic access to all other sectors of national opinion. With the proven support of imperialism, re-actionary forces used all of their powers to recover some of the ground they had lost. On the one hand, they attempted to confiscate the "workers' network" (Channel 9 of the University of Chile) and, on the other, they tried to extend throughout the country Channel 13 (the Catholic University of Santiago's network) which uncon-ditionally supported the seditious movement. Channel 13's director, a priest named Hasbun, now relieved of his function by the Junta, was also the spiritual director of the magazine *Eva*, which we will discuss later.

The mass media became the favourite launching pad for the bourgeois offensive. But in order to fulfil this rôle, the media had to undergo an important change. At the crux of this change was a new conception of who was listening to their messages. The bourgeoisie began to define its audience in terms of the rôle they could play within the counter-revolutionary movement and the particular interests which motivated each section. In other words, its mass political strategy was reflected in the mass media. In order to help agitate and organise their potential constituency, the media's messages were aimed at specific fronts: owners' associations, professional associa-tions (journalists, doctors, lawyers, engineers), youth and, last but not least, women. Between November 1970 and June 1973, *El Mercurio* devoted 120 editorials to the women's movement. Here is a sample which attempts to discredit the social organisation of socialist countries in the eyes of the female public. Under the headline "Women's Brutal Work", this editorial tried to warn "those women workers and employees who, happy to the point of euphoria, were on their way to a political propaganda meeting":

"Only a few of these women will reach management level jobs or positions at a higher level in the bureaucracy; only a very few will benefit from extra food rationing stamps and an extra few yards of material for their homes. And even fewer will be able to work honourably, with due consideration to the weakness of their sex and with enough time to carry out their household and family functions."
(10 November, 1971)

Do we have to say it again? The main impact of the whole terror campaign was aimed primarily at women. The threat which "Marxist totalitarianism" represented for the home, the survival of family ties and the education of children were, and continue to be, the arguments used to stir up world-wide anti-communism. These threats are designed to paralyse women and to push to their limits the conservative features of the dominant feminine culture. In 1964, when Frei was campaigning against Allende, the Christian Democrats broadcast the voice of Juana Castro, a leader in the Cuban exile movement and Fidel's half sister, to convince Chileans to fight communism. In 1970 the same operation was repeated, but with greater violence and a different slant. "Your sons and daughters will be sent to Moscow"; "They will be forced to denounce their parents" read the leaflets. When Fidel Castro announced his visit to Chile, the extreme right-wing publications proclaimed: "The tyrant of the Caribbean is coming to steal the bread from your children's mouths." The ghost of hunger and the spectre of Marxism were slogans that constantly appeared on city walls, in newspapers and on the airwaves. By using this repertoire of arguments and symbols based on mother and child, the right hoped to legitimise the overthrow of the popular government by any means possible: "Your mother is waiting in line... This child cannot wait until 1976! The children of Chile need a solution *now*." The photo to this caption showed a child looking dishevelled and crying in front of his house in a poor neighbourhood.

The bourgeoisie also broke with the traditional format of the women's press in order to further stimulate the active opposition of women. In addition to weekly photonovels and "romance" publications, the Chilean bourgeoisie controlled three magazines. Two were local publications, *Eva* and *Paula*, and the third, *Vanidades*, was really a Panamerican mouthpiece, conceived in Miami but printed in Santiago for national distribution. During the period of the Popular Unity government, these publications still accounted for eighty per cent of the women's press with 200,000 copies printed bi-weekly. The local magazine, *Eva*, originally owned by a group of Christian Democratic publishers, underwent the most spectacular shift. In an interview with foreign journalists, its editor admitted her intention to make it an instrument of agitation. "I have declared war on Popular Unity. Women must fight and we must help them, stimulate them, educate them." A look at the editorials, a few other sections and the many items spread throughout the magazine is enough to convince even the most inexpert reader of its new character – unheard of in a magazine of this type. *Eva* was transformed in two major areas: a welter of intellectual references were cited and all aspects of daily life were politicised. The content remained the same with one important exception. Whereas previously the magazine had rigorously limited its content to sentimentality and love life, the euphoric advertising of modernity, motherly concerns and care for the home, it now introduced items which were supposed to "inform" women about national politics and "open their eyes" to the antagonisms between the two conflicting ways of life. This information was given a female slant. Government and opposition politicians were discredited or praised, according to their physical appearance or their behaviour in private life rather than according to the political programme which they implemented or upheld. The magazine opened its readers to Marx, Lenin and Mao (so they could take on their intellectual adversaries) by focusing on the difficulties suffered by their wives, daughters and *companeras*. At times the magazine preferred to use that classic last resort which the bourgeoisie calls upon to discredit people and systems who reveal the class character of their thinking. It described them as great thinkers and inventors, but figures for the museum of ideas who were irrelevant to present times and conditions. Those actors on the stage of national life who were authorised to appear in *Eva*'s pages as affable, peaceful and "calming" were the representatives of the Armed Forces.

One particular section blatantly contributed to the task of mobilising its readers. It was initiated after the Right was defeated, in the bosses' lockout of October 1972 and continued to appear regularly under the title "Women's Plan for Action". The articles encouraged women to intensify their struggle and even gave them precise instructions. The following is an example from the 23 November, 1972 issue:

"All the military forces in the world train their members. Soldiers train by doing gymnastics, exercising and attending theoretical classes, which helps them to fight: Chilean women should follow this method, which has proved so effective the world over.

"*Gymnastics:* Articles for *Eva* recommend exercises to lose weight and correct figure defects. Gymnastics, however, also fulfil a more important purpose. When a person is healthy, she is agile. With this ability one can carry out more forceful actions, mobilise tirelessly and use time more effectively.

"*Education:* As physical aspects are not enough, the mind also has to be trained. This can be done by reading the newspaper at least three times a week. Women will act more effectively if they know what is going on and what the Communists, Christian Democrats, members of the National Party and the MIR are thinking. You cannot day dream ... Books by John Le Carré, Leon Uris, Vicky Baum also help illustrate the totalitarian methodology ... This intellectual nourishment will clarify why we are struggling.

"*Moral Strength:* We must not forget that sacrifice moulds willpower. It is not logical to invest money in gambling when it is needed for the cause – to keep free radios on the air or to help Channel

13 withstand governmental pressures. We cannot live wars for only a few hours a day. We must remain in the trenches, as an example to others, with sacrifice, engaging in action during the whole day. Women who continue to believe that they need at least five pairs of shoes, more than ten dresses, etc.... are not partaking in this struggle. Women are not active if they do not promote the collection of funds and registration in work groups, whether for social work (*Hogar de Cristo, Mi Casa, La Gota de Leche*, the Red Cross), or political action."

This action plan ended by calling on women to sign up for training in the "regular armies" (the political parties), the "fifth column" (infiltration in the enemy's ranks) or in the guerrilla movement (direct action used against Marxists). As we can see, sedition is a school. Paradoxically, the right-wing's ethics repudiated the frivolous softening of women produced by consumer society, that society which this struggle intended to restore.

This message penetrated the rest of the magazine in a more diffuse fashion, influencing every article dealing with the daily concerns of the housewife. This aspect of right-wing propaganda, while complementary to the one previously mentioned, was perhaps characteristic of the more moderate sectors of the right-wing coalition's strategy for opposition to the popular government. All the recipes, the fashion pages, interior decorating advice, the horoscopes, jokes, humour, every advertisement, every commentary, helped spread the psychosis of hunger and shortages. They helped activate every reflex against the "popular regime" by nurturing a nostalgia for the good old days, by drawing a bleak picture of the future and making the government look inept and the situation unbearable. In the same issue of 23 November, 1972, twenty pages were devoted to food. Recipes and menus based on "products that could be found" in "times of war" were in one column. Recipes and menus of the "good old days" were in the other column. The first part was interspersed with comments such as: "Before, goods could be purchased; now they have to be won by sweating it out in line." Or: "Every day it is harder to be a good housewife." The second part, devoted to the fabulous dishes of the past, was intended to underline the meagreness of the present, and pictured the incredible banquets of the landed oligarchy.

The day after the coup, when the Right flooded the market with the goods it had stockpiled, its newspapers and magazines described the tears of joy shed by housewives at the sight of the renewed abundance. "Chile's second independence" went hand-in-hand with the "liberation of the housewife." And, when the supplies ran out, inflation quickly demonstrated the emptiness of their rhetoric.

3: Giving birth to the gun

In Montevideo, in Uruguay – a country which enjoyed a long, gentle democratic path before falling under the thumb of military dictatorships – military parades have become an everyday event.[1] Today, however, among the lines of parachutists and rangers, one sees detachments of women. Women in uniform march through the streets of Montevideo, rocking in the cradle of their arms a machine gun. If this image springs to mind when looking at the relationship of women to society, it is because, although involving only a very small number of women and distant from our own lived experience, it nonetheless has a profound and far-reaching significance.

One could almost say that this image helps us, by sweeping away all hint of liberal gains, to become brutally aware of the consistent support that society expects from women. In a once free city, women have become wholly integrated into the defence of the military state through the annexation of their womb. Thus is the enormous, dangerous power of reproducing life reduced, recruited and dominated. If this image and this reality are particularly odious, it is because in the end they imply the murder of the deep, carnal woman. In place of the child, a weapon: in place of life, death.

The use of blackmail is familiar to war. The "cheek against cheek" of the mother and child remains the stereotype most frequently used to justify their exorbitant expenditure in the advertising of the aggression industries. The death-producing bureaucracies customarily settle under the ancestral, timeless sign of the woman, procreator of a life that the "lords of war" are duty bound to protect. From an offensive, imperialist action, aggression becomes (through these symbols) a defensive practice. The emblem of the mother and child exorcises its reverse, the widow and the orphan.

This privileged relationship of women to life, a natural function founded in a sacred one, is also invoked as a supreme reason for outlawing all abdication by women of their institutional rôle. The institutions of marriage and the family are protected from the start through the responsibility attached to the rôle of giving birth. "Marriage is truly the creation of a real being", one reads in the doctrine of the Rexists, Nazi collaborators in Belgium. "Divorce consists not only in breaking a contract, but in reality kills a living being."[2] The contract which links women to institutions and to the state operates through this blackmail of life itself. Even outside the extremes of fascist regimes, the guilt fostered among women in relation to children – to whom they never devote enough of their time, enough of their affection – is the daughter of such fears. What myth is more female than that of Danaides? Women will never have finished reproducing life!

One cannot avoid linking this responsibility or destiny defined in terms of biology to the animist conception of the state and state power, and its need to be safeguarded and protected during growth, that one finds among the predecessors of Nazism. Kjellen, the father of Pan-Germanism, whose ideas were to be taken up by the Nazis and then the Latin-American military dictatorships, helps us understand how fascism justifies the legitimacy of expanding the power of the state by comparing it to an organism which needs to live and therefore to develop itself.

"States are conscious and rational beings like man... They have interests, desires, instincts and above all an instinct of conservation, a will to grow, a will to live. If the state is an organism, it needs to grow. The power of the state is a physiological concept."

From this one can begin to see how a shift between the maternal instinct for the conservation of a child's life and the maintenance of order can easily be made. It is without doubt in this thought process that the response of "strong man" regimes to the singularity of women is founded.

The women who march in the streets, gun in hand, escape from being individually enclosed within their homes, a solution constantly emphasised by the authorities. But this escape into the streets is controlled by a supreme authority; the explicit recruitment of bodies is represented by the uniform which carries out – to the benefit of virile values – a flattening of sexual differences. For the androgyny of armies is far from being as impartial as that of walnut trees. If a collective body of women is thus formed, it is as much to drown the emergence of their singularity as to melt it into the totalitarian whole. One could justifiably ask if the spread of uniforms – even beyond these unusual situations – does not always favour masculine authority. Is there not, in all tendencies to uniformity, a return to the power relations which justify authority, where the woman is always lost, always loses out?

These bodies in uniform who march, undifferentiated, unidentifiable, for a more total defence of order, mark the death of a certain idea of femininity. They are, in their own way, an androgynous alternative to the uniformising practices of advertising and fashion, which seek to produce and to reproduce a collective body of women, an undifferentiated shop window feminine body which, in turn, wards off another alternative femininity, that of an unknown and mysterious sex.

To return to the original image, the Montevideo street in which this parade passed is consciously deserted. Everyone has surged to a parallel street where, to protest against a "stolen" future and to express their resistance to an internal occupying force, they indulge in the bizarre activity of window shopping. Why strange? Because the shop windows are half-empty as a result of the re-orientation of the economy towards exports; the purchasing power of the mass of consumers has been severely affected. This pretend shopping therefore becomes a subversive irony and at the same time – hence the intelligence of this form of resistance – behaviour which offers little to the forces of repression (who know only too well that a previous economic system justified and encouraged it). In these two parallel streets, there therefore exists a sort of parabolic transit between two historic moments in the relationship of women to power.

The previous model, which worked its charms through the access of all to consumer goods, situated women as representatives of the middle classes in a sequence whereby security equalled consumption, from which power and dreams were extrapolated. But as the *petit* and middle bourgeoisie, natural targets for this model, but now despoiled by it, are rapidly becoming poorer, other female profiles become necessary. The passage from a consumer economy to one where consumerism is no more than a daily demystified lure, requires other ideologies, other practices than those of a "feminine" security, coiled into the pleasure of the individualist promise of well-being.

The symbolic rape of change

On the screens of most Western television systems at the moment one can see American series, like *Sargent Anderson*,[3] whose heroine is a policewoman. At a time when femininity is escaping from its yoke, the power structure needs to underline the extreme conformity of women. Hence the importance of police rôles to try to forestall the tide. These regulating missions also produce a stilted version of women's liberation. Women come to fulfil a militant function as agent of repression with the same rank as men, but doubly efficient in that they introduce sentimental attitudes into the world of the police. When the legitimacy of order cracks somewhere and authority demands to be plugged, the real recruitment of women in the streets of Montevideo becomes in other contexts, in other states of political development, a polymorphous, symbolic recruitment. There are other ways of assuring control than by putting on uniforms.

For an example of this, let us compare the two versions of *King Kong*, a famous crisis fable in which an appeal to the conformity of women is renewed in the context of mass cultural production. It is hardly surprising that the prologue to the original film (made in the context of the 1930s crisis) was cut. In this prologue, one hears the extraordinary scream of a woman, the language of suspense which passes from one monster to another, from a socio-economic beast to a phantastic giant ape. This cry, which returns to structure the film, anchors in the foreground the social and historical fact which has been determinant in the symbolic creation – the feeling that "everything is falling apart" in the Great Depression, a feeling capable of animating the most archaic phantasms – the Beast, the Fall, the Devouring.

Long rationing queues in the streets of Manhattan. Ann, an unemployed actress, forced to steal an apple from a fruit stall, screams in terror when she is seized by the shopkeeper. Crisis of truth for the fictional woman. Her long, first cry, echoing on to the terrifying body of Kong, evokes our terror of the jungle: civilisation, technology and the state think they have expelled the Beast, concreted the jungle. But the jungle and the Beast are still there.

There was no need for the censor's scissors to mutilate the second version of *King Kong*, released in 1977 as one of the series of disaster films accompanying the present crisis. The new Ann, who will sail towards the island of Kong with businessmen in search of oil, is simply the survivor of a yacht in distress, mythically emerging from the limbo of the sea. From her first appearance, as a sumptuous shipwrecked creature rescued from the deep, she revives traditional feminine mythology which tolerates neither bohemians nor tramps. Her crescendo cry in the face of the Beast becomes the whimpering hysteria of the naïve woman confronted with an enormous phallic mechanism. It is no longer in terms of her own personal response to a crumbling society that she can link herself to a collective imagination, producer of phantasms. The recession is for her no more than a decor without scenes; she will only live in her poor, borrowed phantasms. Unfamiliar with tension or contradiction, naked and stripped of history, the new Ann functions only as a simple place of transit, a libidinous and mystified prop for archaic drives artificially convoked by the crisis. In the same way that Kong is no longer comparable to the body of a monstrous order which was to resolve the crisis of the 1930s through the growth of fascism, the heroine sees herself dispossessed of the intimate and productive relation between a historical lived experience and the creation of phantasms: a sign of a new, much more latent fascism which progresses through the obliteration of the symbols of power and the sterilisation of the cry, a reflex of survival. Is it not literally contradictory that this embryonic discourse, the offspring of resistance contained in the scream of the original version of the film, has not been magnified in the second one, on the basis of the political gains evidenced by the active search of women to become masters of their own discourse?

The meaning encompasses the measure of the contradiction.

"Last hired, first fired", the woman is perhaps the first to be recruited, during times of crisis, by the wave of symbolic violence which attempts to reduce outbreaks of dissidence in order to re-assemble them on the terrain of the forces of order.[4] Through the twilight of the issue, one perceives women's place in the gravitation of ideological control.

This simple comparison between the two versions of the hairy Beast, a fable rediscovered each time chaos strikes, can only give a glimpse of the way in which mass culture, at two different moments of its history, can interpret and live a situation of the same nature, tightening its control over individual and collective digressions which have emerged between the two crises. Even if it means being accused of arbitrariness, why should we not see in these examples – confirmed elsewhere by other signs – a regressive alternative that order is offering to women who, in the meantime, have lived through a decisive stage of their liberation, both on the level of hope and reality? The new position of women, a disorder in which women have newly assumed their rôle, is a part of what the crisis must subdue so as to reaffirm the primordial, the permanent.

Empty shopping baskets, strong arm democracy

Women have long been caught in the seduction of consumption (by extension, waste) which has fixed the advertising image of female happiness and, through this, the happiness of the whole community. Trapped as it is within the limits of an exemplary status, this image succeeded, nevertheless, in paradoxically helping to transfer the whole of the representations and integrate women into modernity.

Ignoring the contribution of women's non-domestic work to the overall system of production, the economic order interprets this escape from the household only as a guarantee of an increased, more narcissistic consumption. The seduction of the world of the commodity, in which the idea of a female being is dissolved, is based on an exaggeration which has its own norms of credibility: an apparently unlimited supply of goods and growth, a guarantee that the future will be more radiant than the present. But the crisis in the economy of abundance transforms this hyperbole into, at best, a stagnant statement. The scarcity of production and capital increases the necessity for ideological re-investments. After having made women the radiant symbols of "affluence" advertising, the keystone for its democracy of desire, the economically sickening order can no longer make the same eclectic offers sparkle, and must try to restore the hegemony of moral values.

The new philosophers of the recession make no mystery of the requirements: a rationalisation of the economy of excess will not occur without a rationalisation of the "excesses of democracy". The expression of "strong man democracy" (a democracy which asserts its sex) clearly depicts the new territory on which order is trying to found its now threatened authority. It was on the subject of *The Godfather*, a film that marked the revival of Hollywood in the 1970s, that one of the intellectual guides of American advertising, one of the best known practitioners of behaviourism, commented:

"The very unpredictability of the world that we live in has made new types of management approaches necessary... Even in the political field, conclusions can be drawn from the success of such films as *The Godfather* and *Godfather II*. One of the most crucial dilemmas that we are likely to be faced with in the future, and which will have immediate consequences for marketing and advertising, will be the dilemma of the authoritarian versus democratic approaches. There is a growing desire for what we euphemistically call strong leadership. Millions of people go to see and enjoy *The Godfather* because we, without admitting it, admire this kind of a much more 'fail safe' organisation of the world."[5]

Thus the principle of authority, increasingly required by the governments of today, organises itself essentially around male values. The film critic of the economic weekly *Valeurs Actuelles* (Current Values), acclaiming these "parables" emerging from the crisis, stated quite bluntly: "These films are a... sudden burst of Western values. They advocate a sort of re-evaluation of values... They exalt essentially virile values."

On 28 August, 1976, in Belfast, 20,000 Protestant and Catholic women courageously defied their antagonists by chanting "Our Father" in the Protestant suburb of the city where, until that day, most Catholics had never set foot. Why, when the women demonstrators of the Peace Movement in Ireland seek, outside the political parties, to make their voices heard on the obvious need for peace and bread, is it also to the Father that they address their prayers? Is it not significant that this demonstration for peace preferred to invoke the Father rather than the Holy Spirit who, in the division of labour of the Holy Trinity, is nevertheless in charge of missions of pacification?

Strong arm regimes, or those lacking authority, are inclined to run off with this dialectic by seeking to legitimise themselves through the seduction exercised on women. As antithetical images of force, women seem to provide the justification for their chauvinist power.

The soldiers of Pinochet, for example, benefited enormously from the demonstrations by right-wing women. The example has, moreover, left a trail... of prayers and powder! In Mexico and Peru, groups of women have come together to demand a secure state at a time when political power hung in the balance. In Puerto Rico, groups of women gathered to protest against the "threat" of the campaign for independence of the island, an American colony since the invasion of 1898.

Exploiting the apocalypse

So that this rallying cry of authority (resubjugation of the weak, re-affirmation of the natural status of submission) can resound in all its urgency and credibility, an exceptional and dramatic conjuncture is needed: the crisis will be disguised as a "catastrophe", for it is a threat that demands a return to the fundamental, to the founding myths.

In its moments of crisis, order founds history in nature. The woman is restored to the preferential vocation assigned to her by nature, a vocation that the dominant structures have never ceased to confirm, even if it has been with more or less liberalism and ambivalence. Mother, wife, guardian, pillar of the moral order. Making use of the apocalypse, banking on fear, the "catastrophic" imposes the return to a constitutive archaism, rehabilitating traditional models of authority and underlining the natural pre-dominance of the male.[6] His musculature, strength, sense of command and decisiveness (naturally virile assets) take up the symbolic relay of money and a privileged relation to capital. The necessary submission of the woman goes hand-in-hand with that of the panicked masses, who experience their powerlessness to govern and demand the return to the values of order which consecrate the presence of the Chief.

Integrating certain aspects of the new feminine world view (determination, independence, sexual emancipation) fiction in-evitably leads these heroines to take refuge in the hands of their natural protector, man, and regroups these stray sheep around the most male of rams. The whole organisation of these fables of the supersonic age tends to produce among the public, shattered by the "sensurround", an unconditional adhesion to the archaic principles of a moral which legitimises itself as being natural to consecrate the return to a retrograde conception of relations of authority. At the centre of this statism, an essential balance is sought which is in fact the necessary imbalance between the masculine and the feminine. Symbolic rape of change. Is it necessary to stress to what extent this attempt founders on the horizon of the "movement" (precisely) of women – voyage, resistance and derision of defunct normalities?

Tension between modernism and regression exists in all the debates accompanying the development of technology, of which the disaster films are both the offspring and guilty conscience. In these films, the technology escapes from its creators like the monster of Frankenstein from his master, in order better to erase its relations with power. This dichotomy between modernism and regression reflects the way in which advanced capitalism resolves the social insertion of new technology, symbolically enclosed within the field of virile values. The more this technology comes to terms with itself as an instrument of domination, the more it symbolically needs a non-aggressive counterpart, a sort of softness to redeem its overwhelming force. False dialectic of menace and protection. A woman whose status as someone to be protected is continually re-validated, compensates for the repressive meaning of technological development as an extension of male force. As long as the system is moving towards a friendly fascism, why not draw, to publicise and sell it, on images of an eternal femininity which gathers like a swarm of bees around the offensive machines? In fact, it is just as if, in order to contain and repress the revolutionary meaning of the development of science and technology, and in order to prevent these productive forces from adopting other paths, order needs to cultivate continuity, as well as the permanence of the values and symbols which orient behaviour and distribute social rôles.

Feminine frenzy and transnational power

Network, a film released in 1977, was not the first to present an analysis of another medium. One remembers the merciless vision of Orson Welles on the irresistible rise of one of the first magnates of the sensational press, Hearst. *Citizen Kane* brilliantly shows how, seeking to construct empires and increase its sales, this press can exercise a pernicious influence on public opinion.

With *Network*, it is to television, the youngest of the modern communications technologies, that the Hollywood cinema of criticism and denunciation devotes a big budget film. Winner of five Oscars and a box office success, this film seems to have fulfilled all expectations. One cannot help noticing that television, justly accused of stealing the cinema's audience, brings them back when it becomes itself the star of a big screen super-production, where it lends itself to an expiatory sacrifice. For *Network* drags the viewer away from home to reveal the sordid, commercial rules by which a certain conception of television is regulated. Analysing the importance of the television phenomenon as a source of leisure in the modern age, the film shows how the new media are devoured by the economic and technological power that controls them – an interesting point of view when one remembers that the director (Sidney Lumet) and the scriptwriter (Paddy Chayefsky) are themselves surely caught up in the web of these controls. This film is produced by United Artists, subsidiary of a vast multinational conglomerate (Transamerica Corporation) which has interests in air traffic and credit as much as in industrialised culture. It is in terms of this contradiction that one must judge the importance – and underline the limits – of the film.

The threat of dismissal hanging over Howard Beale, established presenter of the news on television (his ratings are down), his rise to grace (hypnotised audiences congregate once again around Beale, who has become "the mad prophet of television") and then his death warrant accompanied by the final holocaust (he is killed "live" by pseudo-terrorists paid to take over the control of hysterical crowds) are the episodes which punctuate the denunciation of a television fallen into the hands of the ratings. What matters is to occupy the network, increase audiences, win the merciless battle of competition with other channels. The dictatorship of the clapometer holds sway in contempt of all morality at the UBS network, a fictional name that scarcely masks the initials of the big networks: NBC, ABC and CBS. Here we find denounced, with the efficiency conferred by caricature, the directing principle of a system of production and distribution of television programmes which, from its base in the United States, operates on an international scale.

A debate takes shape around the future of Howard Beale, opposing the "humanist" clan to that of the young turks whose personal ambition coincides with the desire of the UBS bosses substantially to increase their profits. In the first camp, William Holden, the old news chief, concerned with "content" and keeping his distance from the agitation created by the dictates of competition and the market. In the other, Faye Dunaway, caught up in the fever of the ratings and discovering the supreme trick: "commercially" diverting subversive contents in favour of "her TV" – whether the prophecies of a madman, communist tracts or leftist hold-ups.

Beyond this debate, where an outdated humanism offers no worthwhile solution to compete with the voracity of the system, it appears that television, a technology which changes one's relationship to reality, is more than a vehicle for messages. Faye Dunaway, admitting herself that her affair with William Holden is like a television series, is the best example of this McLuhanian "television generation".

But what is hidden by this vision of the media as an all-powerful agent, making and unmaking consciousness? By identifying a single guilty party – television – doesn't *Network* exonerate itself from its own alienation? For it is not only the television but also *Network* which practises the most perfect confusionism: giving the "liberated woman" the image of a hysteric whose methods for achieving power lose nothing in comparison with those of men; showing black protesters abandoning their cause for the lure of money; and presenting the power of the Arabs as an autonomous and overwhelming force on the stage of world capital. Do not the madness of women, the hysteria of the marginalised and the lust of Arabs intervene as diversionary clichés?

Emotional economics

The incredible audience ratings for family sagas on television are another response, another dialectic in the culture of the crisis, another adaptation of mass culture to the reality of the outside world. The home, a space which secures the body within the snare of the system of production and property, becomes, around the television set, the platform for a return to "history", a history conceived in terms of belonging to a lineage, in terms of a voyage back to the original sources, back to the family cradle.

The very title of the most famous of these sagas, *Roots*, could not be more explicit. The triumphal reception this obtained in New York (thus preparing it for massive distribution in other Western countries) is more than symptomatic of the restoration of the family theme as an element of social cohesion; and productions of this type have now displaced all the series (adventure, spies) which have been successful previous models on American television, and therefore assured of a world-wide distribution. By plunging back into former times of slavery and racial discrimination, by reviving the black nationalist vein that generations of the same family live through, *Roots* exorcises, by exalting the epic of the downtrodden, one of the most violent contradictions of the American nation. But if this exorcism was able to reunite the black and white populations of the United States around the life and struggles of the family of Alex Haley (going right back to Africa), it is because the narrative also operates elsewhere. This more existential impact is confirmed by the code of the new *savoir-vivre*, a therapy accompanying the promotion of the new product: "Find your roots. Fight against your feeling of uprootedness".

An essential anchoring point, the family becomes the horizon on which the ethnological itinerary of each and every one is deployed like a form of medication. An exclusive focal point, it expels all attempts to depict or question the external world and its institutions.

The intervention of the latter could only weaken the force of the central theme of this saga, that of the moral fortress represented by the unity of the family, an element of order in the world of disorder, a rock amid the waves of fortune and misfortune. The accent on the self-sufficiency of the family household is in response to the nostalgia for a time before the desire for the emancipation of ages and sexes, a time before divorce, before the collapse of the family, a nostalgia for the time when the woman/family assured the tranquil durability of everyone's rôle in the social structure, serving as a home port for the adult and juvenile expeditions of men. Through this economy of pretences, the domestic enclosure is built up into a small state which removes the guilt of the big state for its insufficiencies, collaborating with institutional society, obliterating once more the presence of power.

In the shadow of the advance of women, other worrying aspects can be observed, and always in the dark continent of mass culture, whose very triviality can be discouraging for many intellectuals. And yet is there not a moment when indifference, or even contempt towards the flood of programmes, weeklies and series which arrive every day in the lived experience and dreams of millions of women, becomes a form of abandonment of the link that Gramsci judged necessary between the intellectuals and the people? (Obviously this doesn't mean that the intellectual alone possesses the key to meaning and that the masses are lacking in critical consciousness.)

The romance magazine is one of those cultural forms whose strange revival, visible today, is more than a little surprising. There are many reasons for thinking that it should be in decline, in the middle of the modern age. The assaults of the advertising machine and the triumphal march of fashion would appear to leave little legitimacy to these photo-novels with their obscure and obscurantist style. What shadowy tendencies explain the fact that, in Europe, France and Italy, both countries ripe to enter another political age, the sentimental press is blossoming, whereas women's magazines, with their reviews of fashion designed for the "modern" woman, are displaying the outward signs of crisis? It is estimated that the "up-market" women's press (*Marie Claire, Marie-France, Elle*) recorded a decline in unit sales of eighteen per cent between 1972 and 1977. New "up-market" titles like *Cosmopolitan*, which sold 238,000 copies in 1978, are trying to win over the 550,000 readers lost by the others. The decline of the "family women's press" was only three per cent; and this crisis was limited to 1974, after which the biggest titles in this category (*Nous Deux, Intimité, Modes et Travaux*), which today sell over three million copies, re-established themselves. Furthermore, it is estimated that, given the recent introduction of the photo-novel in numerous other weeklies (television guides, for example), the monthly circulation of this type of message reaches twenty million copies in France. On top of this, the more one goes "down-market", the more intense is the circulation, as each copy is handed on to others. The case of *Bonne Soirée* reveals the conservative character of these titles: this weekly attempted, following May 1968, to adapt to the times by changing its editorial content. Rue the day! *Bonne Soirée* lost 300,000 readers in six months, readers which it is now trying to recover.[7]

What is striking – and the figures are there to prove it – is the lasting quality of these narratives, which confine disorder within the economy of the heart so as better to cultivate the passion for order, and trace out the desired functions of an instituted morality which can animate the masses, particularly feminine masses, at various moments of their history. It is a conjuncture that the industry of cultural standardisation, evading and ridiculing the contrary, impregnable desire for struggle against the established system, was very early on baptised as a structure so as to be able to qualify these narratives as "popular literature". In an age when society is cracking at the macro-level of power, the legitimacy of the closed discourses of micro-orders is being revived. Through the regulated and repetitive articulation of their sequences, which direct an initial situation of anarchy towards the obligatory restitution of happiness in accordance with the rules, these amorous narratives mesh like so many cogs with the unconscious fascination for order. Marginalising works which do not correspond to what their economy of penury offers to the masses, dictatorships favour large doses of this sub-literature, compatible with the return to the woman as a symbol of a certain idea of family and fatherland, a mystified womb of traditional values.

We have already remarked how, in order to bring these dictatorships to power, latent elements of the dominant women's culture can be cynically manipulated so as to shroud the rise of fascism in legitimacy and innocence. In the streets of Santiago, the "naturally" pacifist and passive character of women, hypnotised by consumption or a love affair, lost its inert façade as a deadweight in political life to become the strongest weapon of the counterrevolution. Once women had taken to the streets, one could see the importance of the ideological and cultural investments made by the dominant order in women.

The night porters

The relationship between women and fascism is not one which has been established once and for all. It is subject to the concrete historical circumstances in which authoritarian regimes arise. In the fascist countries of Latin America today, women no longer take to the streets to acclaim the natural leader that a *duce* or *führer* aspires to be. The recruitment of women in Montevideo has nothing now of the pomp and crowd ritual of European fascisms. This is because, in Uruguay, as in Chile, the history of the last few years – especially for women – has been that of a deception which can no longer be hidden.

Unlike European forms of fascism, which were able to unite a certain social base, the military dictatorships have difficulty in justifying the bare minimum of consensus. The economic system instituted by the juntas, delivering the country to the monopolist bourgeoisie and foreign capital, has quickly dissolved – by impoverishing an expanding *petit bourgeoisie* – those large populist movements in whose favour *chic* women, housewives, and some women in the liberal professions gathered in the streets of Santiago to bang their pots and pans and wave their handkerchiefs.

This "democratic" movement of women and its shock weapon, "women's power" which, shielded by its femininity, was able to demand with impunity the intervention of the he-man – the soldier – to save the strong state, were enjoined to return to their homes once their mission was accomplished. As Brecht remarked: "What is done in the kitchen is not decided in the kitchen". Was it feared that in time these women in the streets would adopt bad habits, like a taste for power, and that the class movement to which they had only lent their support would degenerate into a sex-based movement? The ground rules had, however, been fixed in advance: what real movement for women's emancipation would have adopted the pot as its symbol, the ancestral emblem of women's subjection? Today, the pot, in its evocative value of the legitimate concerns of the housewife, betrays only too well the trickery of which many of these women have been the object.

The concept of "national security" is well known from MacCarthyist current in the United States (the expression "witch-hunt", popularised at the time, shows immediately the way in which "subversive" and female are identified). Now the Latin American generals have contributed their own tradition, mixing allegiance to the old notions of Iberian fascism, saturated with an ultramontane fundamentalist church, with the modern need to integrate themselves into the geopolitics of the great Northern empire by espousing the technocratic contours of its doctrine of expansion. It is still the case that "national security" has no other goal than to guarantee the realisation of national objectives against a clearly identified internal and external enemy: communism.

Total war is declared, dividing the world into two blocs and implying, in each country, that every citizen exists only as a soldier of the nation. All the spheres of everyday life are mobilised by military norms which make everyone, through their gestures and actions, the guarantor of national security, the agent of combat against subversion, a notion sufficiently vague as to allow any definition.

Hitler designated the woman as a "soldier of everyday life". Her militarisation in the ranks of the forces of order is only, in effect, the explicit, spectacular version of her everyday recruitment in the new organisation of reality. Her field of battle – ordinary, banal – remains that of the domestic space.

Two missions are expected of her: to educate her children in the cult of the country and to supervise the family budget in terms of the requirements of the national economy. Pinochet himself updates the accents of the *duce* or *führer*: "Chile needs the technical contribution of its professionals, but does not, for all that, underestimate the anonymous work of women who, in the silent laboratory of the household, supervise the most precious capital of the nation: the education of their children, future hope of the country."[8] The rigorous discrimination of masculine/feminine, private/public, production/consumption rôles has never been so clear:

"The regulation of family consumption is the responsibility of women, whereas production corresponds to men. As a wife and mother, it is the woman who creates the household habits; it is for her to encourage or stop a fashion or a superfluous expenditure."[9]

The order of the day is for sacrifices, privation and frustration. The mystical compensation for this is "the satisfaction of preventing communism from returning to establish itself in this land."

To underline the priority of the domestic rôle of women – and give value to her participation in the struggle against inflation on the basis of her sacrifices – the authorities do not hesitate openly to refute the active rôle played by women in the ranks of the counter-revolution. This was described as exceptional and, on the occasion of the ceremonies for the Year of Women, it was indicated to what extent their political activity had transgressed sexual norms:

"Under the Marxist government, women performed unnatural tasks like defending the freedom of education of their children, freedom of expression and freedom of provision ... Under the present regime, they have returned to their transcendental rôle of supervising family resources."[10]

One should note that the maternal vocation of women is stressed as the very guarantee of their adhesion to nationalist values. "With their family instinct, women picked up better than anyone the evil affecting Chile. They unmasked the enemy of the Chileans". The mission given to them henceforth is quite logically that of "remedying the crisis of values suffered by the nation" and "spreading nationalist values".

The confinement of women to the home breaks the rising tradition of access of women from the petty bourgeoisie to secondary and university teaching and the public service. It inevitably has a particular effect on the lower classes, as is witnessed by circulars from the Ministry of Education dissuading girls from outlying suburbs from continuing their studies, "hairdressing courses being more important for their future than a school curriculum". Specialist colleges have been opened to organise the training of working-class girls "destined" to be servants, whereas for all women, the civil service has handed over the responsibility for the technical learning of the functions of schoolmistress and housewife to the army. Here, technology reinforces traditional rôles: an indication of the mixture of archaism and modernism that characterizes third world fascism.

The formal militarisation of women, incorporated under the colours, completes a plan whose intention is clearly, through technical planning, to contain all the possible outbursts of liberal "femininity": the discourses bear witness to the extent to which the authorities distrust the latter... just as the Nazis interpreted the emancipation of women as a pure product of Jewish intellectualism.[11] "The training of women cannot be left to chance." The nature of women has been invoked as a guarantee of the security of the household and the nation: nevertheless, order takes every precaution against the unbridling of this nature.

The fertility of the womb is no longer the object of a cult in the new latitudes of fascism. The repression of the body-for-oneself now obeys other reasons of state. Even if public homages continue to be rendered to mothers of large families, heroines of the struggle against inflation, the accent is no longer put on the need to procreate. The population policy finds itself, in effect, at a contradictory junction between old ultramontane principles, bitterly opposed to birth control (they still inspire the slogans of the "right to life"), and the geopolitics of imperialism, which seek to reduce the number of children in the lower classes, procreators of the "internal enemy". National security chooses to proceed through the purification of the underdeveloped genes of certain ethnic groups, seen as a fertile terrain for communism. Vast sterilisation plans for working-class women are in process. However, on this point, Chile is still far removed from Guatemala or Puerto Rico, where mass sterilisations carried out without the women's consent drain the threat of a real genocide.

This defiance of the "popular", an expression of the social and ideological racism which excludes (from Chileaness, "Hispanishness" or the "Imperium") the native, the popular, the proletarian, all variants of the non-human, finds in the woman, guardian of the species, a choice victim. To serve the new state, the popular must be tamed. Just as in pre-industrial England, Malthus ascribed the misery of proletarians to their lack of concern and their disorganised fertility, today working-class mothers are blamed for bad child nutrition, "an endemic evil due in large part to their incompetence and ignorance". "They must be educated." This justifies all the practices of indoctrinating women. The justification of this is scandalous when one remembers that under Allende their ingenuity worked wonders.

A political dissident, the woman is doubly punished because she is doubly subversive, doubly sorceress. The demonisation of all non-conformist forces finds in her its primary expiatory target. The only form of femininity with rights to the city, or rather the barracks, in these garrison states is that under the alibi of which the armed wing of the plot was unleashed. The funereal misogyny expressed in the tortures reserved for alternative forms of femininity shows the willingness to kill the purest defiance of masculine authority crystallised in the strong state of military dictatorships.

The exile of possible forms of femininity from ideologies of order has perhaps never been so clearly expressed as by Alexandre Dumas: "We shall say nothing about the Communard bitches (*femelles*) out of respect for the women they resemble when they are dead."

Notes and references

PART I: EVERYDAY LIFE

1: From soap to serial
1. Miles David and Kenneth Costa. "Since 1895, radio finds its niche in the media world", *Advertising Age*, 19 April, 1976.
2. The advertising revenue of commercial radio stations in the United States was soon to become very high and sponsors used to take over part of a programme and organise it as they saw fit. The volume of advertising revenue made it possible to launch some very ambitious programmes. Certain sections of the public soon expressed concern at the increasing impact of advertising on radio broadcasting; and a motion for reducing this impact was tabled in the senate as early as 1936. Information assembled in Pierre Miquel's *Histoire de la radio et de la télévision*, Paris, Editions Richelieu, 1972.
3. Information assembled in René Duval's *Histoire de la radio en France*, Paris, Editions Alain Moreau, 1979.
4. Rodolfo Stavenhagen, "Invisible women", *Unesco Courier*, July, 1980. Many women and many women's associations have studied this problem. Cf. Rosalyn Baxandall, Elizabeth Ewen and Linda Gordon. "The working class has two sexes", in *Monthly Review*, Vol. 28, No. 3, July–August, 1976. See also the articles in the "Special Issue on the Continuing Subordination of Women in the Development Process", *IDS Bulletin*, April, 1979, Vol. 10, No. 3, University of Sussex. Reference may also be made to Harry Braverman, *Labour and Monopoly Capitalism*, New York, Monthly Review Press, 1974, and above all to the study which must be considered as the classic monograph on the subject, namely Mariarosa Dalla Costa, "Donne e sovversione sociale" (Italian title), translated into English as "Women and the Subversion of the Community", in *The Power of Women and the Subversion of the Community*, Bristol, Falling Wall Press, 1972.
5. Isabel Larguia and John Dumoulin, "Toward a science of women's liberation", New York, North American Congress on Latin America (NACLA), *Latin America and Empire Report*, No. 6.
6. This confirms the Latinity of the genre. With regard to this Latinity, it would be interesting to study the particular moment at which, in individual countries, this type of serial was introduced into programme schedules, and to try to determine whether it is descended from earlier forms of expression (literature, the press, cinema), in order thereby to assess to what extent it corresponds to particular trends in specific socio-cultural environments. It is here that one feels the absence of historical studies which might show how one genre is descended from another, and trace the gradual development of certain forms of traditional culture towards forms of mass culture.
7. Mexico, a vital link in transnational publishing in Latin America, also has a large national output of photo-novels and romance magazines. The same is true of Argentina and Brazil. In all these countries production is professional and industrial, whereas in Colombia it is still very artisanal.
8. In 1979, Harlequin Enterprises, leader of the "romance" novel publishers, declared its intention to set up a publishing empire in the United States. It began by acquiring the Laufer company, which publishes *Tiger Beat*, several magazines for adolescents and, above all, the Rona Barret gossip magazines. Cf. *Who owns the media?*, edited by Benjamin M. Compaine, New York, Harmony Books, 1979.

9. See A. and M. Mattelart, X. Delcourt, *International Image Markets*, Comedia, London, 1984.
10. Cf. Michèle Mattelart, *La cultura de la opresion feminina*, Mexico, Editorial Era, 1977; Anne-Marie Dardigna, *La presse féminine*, Paris, Maspero, 1978; Cornelia Butler Flora and Jan L. Flora, "The *fotonovela* as a tool for class and cultural domination" in *Latin American Perspectives*, special issue entitled "Culture in the age of mass media", Issue 16, Vol. V, No. 1, Winter, 1978.
11. Alexandra Kollontaï, *Marxisme et Révolution sexuelle*, Paris, Petite Collection Maspero, 1977.

2: Women as consumers

1. M. Mattelart, "Chile: political formation and the critical reading of television", in *Communication & Class Struggle*, International General Editions, New York, 1983. Countries with a socialist orientation know how difficult it is to do away with serialised TV melodramas, which have a broad public appeal. In Chile, under Allende, Channel 9 decided to use the serial entitled *Simplemente Maria* to entice viewers into watching the news programme which followed. The government of Nicaragua, faced with popular discontent over the disappearance of TV "novels", decided to re-introduce them. In Mozambique, a similar problem has arisen over Indian melodramas.
2. The critic Robert Grelier described the film in the following terms in *La Revue du Cinéma* (No. 320–321, October, 1977): "A film with three central pivots – the exploiting landlord, the 'madman' and the peasants – *The 3,000-year Harvest* draws its inspiration from a song which has given the film its title and is heard three times. The words of the song are as follows: 'Our bride, our new bride, your bridal gown has never been torn in all its 3,000 years'. It inspires the dream of the young peasant helping his father with the plough and is repeated as a theme song throughout the film. This poor land, still with its feudal structures, is depicted without condescension or compassion, but with much nobility of spirit. The sweat and the fatigue appear on the peasants' faces like stigmata of the exploitation they are suffering. The spoken word does not pervade the whole film but lets the image follow its own course. People speak only when necessary. Sounds, i.e. noises, are given the place they deserve, the place they enjoy in everyday life. Oral traditions, dreams, allegories and symbols are used by the director as active elements linked to this documentary vision but never as pretexts for aestheticism or for embellishing the form of the work, whose principal quality resides in the sobriety of the images. Time and technology, like the cloud of dust in which a convoy of lorries is just visible, pass through this landscape but never stop. Omnipresent traditions preserve the privileges which may be in the process of changing; but it seems that a price will have to be paid, and that the class relationships which govern this society will have to be tackled sooner or later. These relationships are merely hinted at in the lines spoken by 'madman' but are not evident to most of the protagonists."
3. The melodrama is the principal genre in the commercial cinema in India. In India today, the cinema is a major means of mass communication. The country ranks as first in the world for the production of films: the 714 films produced in 1980 (seventy-two per cent of them in colour) were seen by three billion people. Television, on the other hand, is still in its infancy: its sixteen channels, in black and white, only cover twelve per cent of the country and its programmes are viewed by less than eight per cent of the population (about 600,000 households own a television set). (Source: *La Monde Diplomatique*, March, 1981.)
   Many of these commercial films (which contain a mixture of songs, mythology, violence, humour, dancing and tears and suffering, and feature popular stars idolised by the masses) are exported to Africa, both black Africa and the Maghreb. A country such as Mozambique has still to come to terms with

the fascination exercised on its urban population by Indian melodramas. The proportion of Indian films imported into Mozambique is still very large, large enough indeed to maintain the dominating position which such films have enjoyed in the past (a domination of the market which they share with Karate films from Hong Kong, another major film production and distribution centre for Africa). Of the 714 films imported in 1976, 223 – approximately a third of the total – came from India, 122 from the United States, ninety-eight from Italy, sixty-four from France and forty-nine from the Soviet Union and other countries. (It is clear, therefore, that these Indian films are much more popular than North American westerns and comedies.) Today, Mozambique is pursuing a policy of diversification with regard to imports of films. Out of 162 new films imported in 1980 from twenty-three different countries, there were still thirteen from India, but half of these had been made by progressive film directors who have set themselves apart from the mainstream of commercial films in India. There are, in fact, increasing signs of the emergence in India of a local and realistic school of cinema, of a high standard, which is modifying in a progressive direction the basic premises of the melodrama. Egypt is another major production centre for romantic films, which are mostly exported to Middle-Eastern countries.

4. Cf. the mimeographed study entitled *Understanding and Use of Educational Films in Villages in Tanzania*, by M. Leveri, P. Magongo, S. Mbungira and J. Siceloff, presented to the Audio-Visual Institute, Dar-es-Salaam, in February, 1978. The villagers expressed their preference for a linear montage of the shots taken, and for a pace of shooting which would make it possible to illustrate in every detail, and with all its natural slowness, the process of manufacturing objects or performing certain tasks. Also, they clearly wanted the theme of work to be related to the themes of everyday family and community life.

3: *Information* versus *fiction*

1. *The influence of audio-visual media on the socio-cultural behaviour of women. Two examples: Japan and Canada*, (Cultural Development: Documentary dossier 17), Unesco, 1980. This section of the study was written by Yoko Nuita, Director of the National Centre for the Education of Women.
2. In France, this is the case with magazines such as *Bonne Soirée, Confidences, Modes de Paris* and others.
3. Pierre Bourdieu has demonstrated that "public opinion" is, in fact, an illusion. Cf. P. Bourdieu, "L'opinion publique n'existe pas" in *Les Temps Modernes*, Paris, No. 318, January, 1973.
4. Henri Lefèbvre, *Le manifeste différentialiste*, Paris, Gallimard, "Idées", 1970. In this line of thought, it may be mentioned that commercial networks, which are governed less by the public interest and public morality, may often display more laxity than public networks. This is what the Japanese author means when she states that: "a number of television programmes broadcast in the daytime by private television networks a few years ago used to depict adultery or illicit sexual relations. They were criticised for this."
5. Anne Légaré, "Le cas de l'émission 'Femme d'aujourd'hui', (Canada)", in *The influence of audio-visual media*, op. cit.
6. Any questioning of the genre introduces a destabilising factor into the communications order. We have in the past noted how a communications policy which attempts to redefine the relationship between the media and their audiences always comes up against this compartmentalisation into genres, which serves to divide and rule. Cf. the analysis of the problem of genres in "Continuity and discontinuity", "Communications: Points for a polemic", by Armand and Michèle Mattelart, which appears in A. Mattelart, *Mass Media, Idéologies and the Revolutionary Movement*, 1980, The Harvester Press (Sussex), Humanities Press (New Jersey), pp. 93–146.

PART II: MODERNITY

1: The feminine ideal

1. Mr Brzezinski has provided us with his version of the reasons why the United States is in the forefront of innovation in the world. In spite of the self-congratulatory and decidedly boastful tone, his remarks are interesting: "The higher the level of per capita income in a country, the more applicable seems the term 'Americanisation'." This indicates that the external forms of characteristic contemporary American behaviour are not so much culturally determined as they are an expression of a certain level of urban, technical, and economic development. Nonetheless, to the extent that these forms were first applied in America and then "exported" abroad, they became symbolic of the American impact and of the innovation-emulation relationship prevailing between America and the rest of the world. "What makes America unique in our time is that confrontation with the new is part of the daily American experience. For better or worse, the rest of the world learns what is in store for it by observing what happens in the United States." From *Between Two Ages: America's rôle in the technetronic era*, Penguin Books, 1970, p. 31.

2. *Cosmopolitan* was introduced in France in December, 1973. It is modelled on the Hearst group publication of the same name. It occupies a specific niche in the market and seems to be scorned by middle-class women. Nevertheless, *Cosmopolitan* is holding its own on the French market, with an average circulation of 193,000 copies per issue, against 302,000 for *Elle* and over 500,000 for both *Marie-Claire* and *Marie-France*, which will dominate the market.

3. Another women's magazine designed for young readers, also based on an American model duly tested on the market, is *Jacinte*, launched in September, 1975. It resembles popular magazines in the United States such as *Glamour*, *Seventeen*, and *Mademoiselle*, which have a combined circulation of four million each month. Cf. Armand and Michèle Mattelart, *De l'Usage des Médias en Temps de Crise*, Paris, Editions Alain Moreau, 1979.

4. Quoted in Stuart Ewen, *Captains of Consciousness*, New York, McGraw Hill Books, 1976.

5. In the mid-1880s, James Walter Thompson, the founder of the first North American advertising agency, was the first to realise the advertising potential of women's magazines. He thus became the first to identify the housewife as a centre for the dissemination of the ideology of consumption. In his later years this American advertising pioneer was fond of reciting an old verse which he claimed had influenced his decision to become a women's magazine specialist: "God bless our wives/They fill our lives/With little bees and honey./They smooth life's shocks/They mend our socks/But don't they spend the money!" It was only a mischievous little ditty, but J. W. T. insisted, in his memoirs (published in a special issue of *Advertising Age* devoted to the 100th anniversary of the J. W. T. firm in 1964), that it was "characteristic of the new spirit that was to take possession of American business that this young advertiser got his original inspiration that led to large success from that old rhyme . . . 'But don't they spend the money!' That last point he seized upon. The women spend the money, and to reach the women, one must enter the family. And to reach the family hearth, the new advertising agent turned to the magazines. He noticed that these publications were bought at the news stands to be carried home, or subscribed to directly from the family circle. There the publication lived for thirty days. The young man was amazed that the business and publishing world had hitherto failed to grasp the possibilities of such a medium in the advertising business."

   James Walter Thompson chose to launch his campaigns in two Philadelphia women's magazines which were major publications at the time: *Godey's Ladies' Book* and *Peterson's Magazine*.

Ladies' Home Journal, a women's magazine which was later to become very popular, was introduced by the Curtis group in 1883. By 1900, it had a circulation of one million in the United States.

6. Advertising agents occasionally reveal quite frankly how they adapt their strategies to changes in motivation structures. The concept of creativity is closely related to the climate created by the suffragettes' movement in the 1920s. The following confession by an advertising agent is revealing: "In a free enterprise economy, we have to develop the need for new products. And to do that we have to liberate women to desire these new products. We help them rediscover that homemaking is more creative than to compete with men ... The client wants to sell pie-mix. The woman has to want to stay in the kitchen – and we show him how to do it in the right way. If he tells her that all she can be is a wife and mother, she will spit in his face. But we show him how to tell her that it's creative to be in the kitchen. We liberate her need to be creative in the kitchen." (Quoted in Betty Friedan, *The Feminine Mystique*, New York, Dell Publishing Co., 1963, p. 217.)

7. See Stuart Ewen's analyses in *Captains of Consciousness*, op. cit., in which he coins the term "new patriarchs" to designate the form of control exercised by industrial firms.

8. Figures given by Alva Myrdal and Viola Klein in *Women's Two Rôles – Home and Work*, London, 1956 (quoted in Betty Friedan, op. cit.).

9. Figures given by Theodore Laplow, *The Sociology of Work*, 1954, and the National Manpower Council, *Womanpower*, New York, 1957 (quoted in Betty Friedan, op. cit.)

10. Cf. Jean-Marie Piemme, *La Propagande Inavouée*, Paris, 1975, Coll. 10/18.

11. Anne-Marie Dardigna, *La presse "féminine", Fonction Idéologique*, op. cit.

12. *Elle*, No. 1351, quoted in A. M. Dardigna, op. cit.

13. *Media Decisions*, Vol. II, No. 2, New York, February, 1976.

14. Rosalind Coward, "Sexual liberation and the family", in *M/F*, No. 1, 1978, England.

15. *F Magazine* seems to cultivate this form of snobbery deliberately. The newspaper *Liberation*, in June, 1981, criticised an advertisement that *F Magazine* had placed in *Stratégie* magazine to attract advertisers with an entire page devoted to descriptions of what its readers won't buy, because they don't like it, and another page describing what they will buy. *F Magazine* readers don't like common consumer items. These "dear" ladies prefer to buy all that is dear. Washing powders don't interest them. They have dishwashers, but are allergic to anything remotely related to dirty clothes. They don't drink table wine or beer out of litre bottles – but champagne and imported beer. Soda pop is too common; they prefer Schweppes. They don't dust: they have vacuum cleaners. They don't grind their own coffee: they have expresso machines. Cheese cubes are deemed more elegant party fare than sardines. They also like frozen foods, silver table services, and ketchup. But how on earth are they going to cook their canned vegetables if they don't like saucepans? Perhaps they have cooks to take care of these menial tasks for them....

16. An electronic components assembly worker in North America earns between $3.10 and $5.00 an hour. For the same work in most third world countries, women earn between $3.00 – $5.50 *a day*. According to *Business Asia*, the hourly wage for unskilled labour is fifty-five cents in Hong Kong, fifty-two cents in South Korea, thirty-two cents in the Philippines, and seventeen cents in Indonesia.

17. Cf., for example, Susan S. Green, *Silicon Valley's Women Workers: a theoretical analysis of sex-segregation in the Electronics Industry Labor Market*, Hawaii, East-West Center, 1980; a Santo Domingo women's group, *Mujeres dominicanas, obreras de zona franca*, Santo Domingo, SEP-CUMS, 1979; and the Haitian women's liberation movement (MHLF). "Enquête sur les femmes ouvrières dans l'industrie de sous-traitance", 1979 (mimeographed document).

2: The myth of modernity

1. We could cite many examples of the way in which the message is fixed within an exclusive and excluding atmosphere. The norm is that of a particular class. The experiences of other groups are negated. A few headings should suffice: "The joys of the indispensable daily bath"; "Prolong the delights of your morning bath", etc.

2. Michèle Mattelart: "El nivel mitico de la prensa seudoamorosa", *Cuadernos de la Realidad Nacional*, 3, 1970, Santiago de Chile. (Also published in: Michèle Mattelart, *La cultura de la opresión femenina*, Editorial Era, Mexico, 1977.) (Translator's note: The author is making a distinction between the "romance magazine" in Spanish *fotonovelas* (photo-novels), a common genre in Europe and Latin America, which are generally composed of sentimental stories, illustrated by photographs: a kind of "soap opera" in print, and "women's magazines" (*revistas femeninas illustradas*) which combine fashion, stories, recipes and news items.)

3. See our remarks about the duality of the female market in Part I, Section 1.

4. We find the same phenomenon in "erotic" magazines. A quick survey of the non-linguistic material (pictures, photos) of various magazines of this type reveals that the presence of eroticism follows differential lines and adheres to a dichotomy of taste and culture which we have just pointed out. The *Playboy*-style magazines represent the height of sophistication and refinement of the metropolitan modern sphere, while the others evade foreign mediation and satisfy popular taste in the matter, leaving the photos of blond foreign nudity for the "Sunday" consumption of proletarians.

5. Jean Baudrillard, "La morale des objets" in *Communications* (Paris), 13.

6. In the days following the *coup d'état* of 11 September, 1973, Victor Jara was arrested at the Universidad Tecnica de Santiago and imprisoned in the National Stadium. As he sang to boost revolutionary morale, accompanying himself on the guitar, his hands were cut off by the military in front of his fellow prisoners. He met his death soon after.

7. *Marx and Engels on Literature and Art*, L. Baxandall, S. Morawski, eds., New York, International General, 1974, p. 52.

8. Edgar Morin, preface to Cadet and Cathelat, *La Publicité*, Paris, Payot, 1968.

PART III: CRISES

1: The media and revolutionary crisis

1. Papelera (Paper and Box Manufacturing Company), controlled by the conservative Alessandri family, was the largest pulp and paper company in Latin America and turned out much of Chile's newsprint. During most of the three years of UP government, the Left demanded that the company be nationalised, since it was such a strategic industry. The Right claimed that Allende had destroyed "freedom of the press" in Chile by even suggesting nationalisation. In the end, Papelera was never nationalised, but it did become a rallying point for opposition forces both inside Chile and among the bourgeois forces abroad. Crown Zellerbach held a minority interest in Papelera.

2. Several studies have wrongly attributed the development of all the mechanisms of resistance displayed by the Chilean bourgeoisie at the level of journalistic discourse to the assistance of psychological war experts from the United States. However, it must be stressed that a national class, despite the context of a dependant society and even if it needs the logistic support of the "Empire", is perfectly capable of producing the mechanisms for its survival. Interpretations which isolate the responsibility and initiative of manoeuvres to an external force also favour, on the Left, convenient ways for covering up their own errors. An example of this type of study is the article by F. Landis, "CIA in Chile

Psychological Warfare", *Liberation*, New York, Vol. 19, No. 3, March–April, 1975.

3. This analysis was produced in Santiago just after October, 1972. The first version in Spanish was written by M. Mattelart and the Argentine researcher Mabel Piccini, now exiled in Mexico.

4. Corporatism is a particular ideological and organisational form which is associated with fascism, particularly as it developed in Portugal and Italy. The concept derives from the medieval guilds or "corporations", and not modern business corporations. Economic life under corporatist states was divided into numerous areas (twenty-two in Italy), with a corporation established in each area. These areas might be composed of the military, employers, merchants, workers, professionals, peasants, etc. All "corporations" were under the control of a very strong state apparatus. Corporatist ideology is highly complex, containing residues of feudal ideology, the nostalgia of *petit bourgeois* producers for artisan-like production in the face of increasing industrialisation and proletarianisation, the concept of class collaboration between "equal partners" working together under the arbitration of a powerful state, etc. For a fuller discussion of corporatism and fascism, see Nicos Poulantzas, *Fascism and Dictatorship: The Third International and the Problems of Fascism*, London, New Left Books, 1974, 165–167 ff.

5. *La Tribuna*, organ of the extreme Right, 27 October, 1972.

6. *Poder Femenino* (Women's Power) was the main right-wing women's organisation formed after Allende's election to mobilise women into militant actions against the government. Its leadership and programme were drawn from Fatherland and Liberty and the National Party.

7. Here, as elsewhere, the parties of the Left were outflanked by the popular movement, which created its own organisations, thus provoking a conflict with existing trade unions. One of the great lessons of October was the recognition that neither parties of the Left nor the Right could give direction, revolutionary or counter-revolutionary, to their militants.

8. If the October crisis reinforced the advance of the popular movement, it ended, at government level, in an alliance with the armed forces, who supplied several ministers.

9. The American model of radio prevailed in Chile: only five national stations and a multitude of local or regional stations belonging to private interests.

10. This station was closed by the Junta a year and a half after the *coup*, a sign of the shift in alliances.

11. Under the military Junta, the rate of inflation was to reach over 400%.

12. It was on 21 October, in the middle of the crisis, that the Right succeeded in negotiating a law on arms which was to enable, from June 1973, systematic searches in factories. These searches were carried out with uncommon violence.

13. The JAPs – Juntas de Abasterimiento y Precios (Supply and Price Committees) – were set up all over the country, generally by housewives themselves and local popular organisations, to check that traders were not charging above official prices, nor hoarding. In areas where the Left was strong, the JAPs often took charge directly of the distribution of basic commodities, not infrequently uncovering large stocks of hoarded goods kept by traders as part of the general right-wing campaign of economic destabilisation.

14. Investigations by the US Senate were to discover that millions of dollars had been embezzled by corporatist leaders during the strike.

15. The legislative elections of 4 March, 1973, which Popular Unity won with forty-four per cent of the vote.

2: The feminine side of the coup
1. "The Brazillian Connection", *Washington Post*, 6 January, 1974.
2. *El Mercurio*, 23 September, 1973.

3. In General Pinochet's declaration of principles (11 March, 1974), the issue of a "Parliament" was no longer raised. On the other hand, General Leigh, in January, 1974, attacked a programme produced for Chilean television by a group of women who actively participated in the opposition movement against Allende. The women, it seems, had accused Chilean men of being somewhat "lily-livered".

4. Since women were given the right to vote in Chile, men and women have voted at separate booths, and their votes are tallied separately. Thus, these figures represent actual voting statistics and not projections from public opinion polls. In 1964 the great majority of women (sixty-three per cent) supported the candidacy of Frei. At that time Allende won only thirty-two per cent of the women's vote, against forty-six per cent of the men's.

5. To commemorate this event, the Junta decided to proclaim 26 June as the "Day of The Working Woman". One observation must be made, however. We must be careful not to give the participation of working-class women in the bosses' strike – and, therefore, in the counter-revolution organised by the Right – a numerical importance which it simply did not have. It is estimated that, of a total of 50,000 workers at El Teniente mine, only 5,000 white and blue collar workers followed the strike order issued by the opposition. The number of strikers' wives, sisters or daughters who marched on Santiago on 24 June, 1973, was no greater than the total number of strikers. Although it is not our intention in this article to analyse the Popular Unity's mobilisation of women, one aspect of it must be clarified: when the Left organised women's demonstrations in order to respond to the Right, they were not as spectacular nor did they assemble as many people as those of the Right. But working-class women participated with exemplary enthusiasm and combativeness in the Left's demonstrations, which were organised without discrimination by sex, always bringing together a more or less equal number of men and women.

6. The closest translation of "gremialista" is "corporatist". The women usurped the title under which their husbands participated in the general management set into action by corporations, truckers, doctors, etc.

7. Song of the folk-singing group, Quilapayun, "The Right Has Two Pots".

8. *El Mercurio*, 4 September, 1973.

9. For more on the Chilean bourgeoisie's "mass line", see A. Mattelart, *Mass Media, Ideologies and the Revolutionary Movement*, op. cit.

10. Excerpt from the speech given by the wife of the president of the military Junta to the "Mothers of Chile". Published in *La Tercera de la Hora*, Santiago, Chile, 23 September, 1973.

11. Statement published in *El Mercurio*, 14 September, 1973.

12. Emile Poirier, *Chile and the Panamerican Experience*, Buffalo, 1901.

13. The "emancipation" of ruling-class Chilean women rests, in fact, on the exploitation of poor women who migrate from rural areas. One hundred per cent of ruling-class women who work have maids, thirty per cent had at least two maids in 1968. Even when these women do not work they have maids: in 1968, eighty-five per cent of non-working married women had at least one maid, in the *petit-bourgeoisie*, eighty-eight per cent of working women are helped in their household tasks, but only forty per cent of those who do not work have help. For more information on the situation of women in Chile before the Popular Unity government, see Armand and Michèle Mattelart, *La mujer Chilena en una nueva sociedad*, an investigative study on the situation and image of women in Chile (Santiago, Chile: Editorial el Pacifico), 1968. Vania Bambirra deals with aspects of this question for the subsequent period in two articles: "La mujer Chilena en la transicion al socialismo," *Punto Final*, Santiago, Chile, 22 June, 1971, and "Liberacion de la mujer y lucha de clases", *Punto Final*, February, 1972.

14. Women were given the right to enter university in 1877.

15. *Eva* (Santiago, Chile), January, 1974.

16. By offering women the opportunity to obtain real popular power, the JAPs mark

the starting point of a movement for women's emancipation and participation. Women of the shanty-towns began to support the Left in direct struggle against the bourgeoisie, particularly around issues of community organisation. They began to demand that health clinics be set up in shanty-towns and were trained as medics and doctor-helpers. They participated in vaccination campaigns, sanitation control and the teaching of preventive medicine. From the Ministry of Education they demanded schools and overcame material scarcity by proposing that old buses be converted into classrooms.

The UP government proposed to create a Ministry of the Family and did develop a national women's organisation, the Patriotic Women's Front, to deal with the problems of women's participation in the political process. The effectiveness and scope of these measures, however, were limited. This was due, in part, to the fact that women were not incorporated into the production process in any great numbers, so that the material basis of their marginalisation was not challenged.

17. The right wing women's organisations and parties ceaselessly proselytised these women. It was common to hear leisure-class women in their forties comment to each other: "So and so called me up," or "So and so invited me to a meeting," etc. There is a great similarity between the tactics used by the Balaguer regime in the Dominican Republic and those of the Chilean Right. It is not by chance that these tactics are based on mechanisms of participation similar to those instituted by the Christian Democrats in Chile and are based on the same conception of women's rôle in the society. Moreover, the theorists of Chilean Christian Democracy participated in the planning of the so-called Cruzada del Amor (Crusade of Love) to organise women after the US invasion. See "Feminismo Balaguerista: A Strategy of the Right", *NACLA's Latin America & Empire Report*, Vol. VIII, No. 6, April, 1974.

18. See M. Mattelart, "Chile: political formation and the critical reading of television", op. cit. See also Michèle Mattelart and Mabel Piccini, "La televisión y los sectores populares", *Communicación y Cultura*, Buenos Aires, 2, 1974, pp. 3–75.

3: Giving birth to the gun

1. This essay was written in 1977.
2. The Rexists were collaborators with the Nazi occupiers of Belgium. Quoted in *Cahiers du Grif*, 14–15, December, 1976.
3. In 1976, three new women police programmes appeared in the United States: *Police Woman*, *Amy Prentiss* and *Get Christie Love*. One should also add the multiplication of "superwoman" characters, a different version of policewomen.
4. "The woman at home: a remedy to unemployment?" was painted on the walls of a factory being occupied by women workers opposed to being laid off (seen on French television channel TF1, July, 1977).
5. E. Dichter, in *Advertising Age*, 5 January, 1976.
6. Our analysis is based on a range of productions in the disaster film category, including *Towering Inferno*, *Earthquake*, *The Poseidon Adventure*, *Jaws*, etc.
7. See the two dossiers published in *Le Journal de la presse*, May and June, 1978, on the women's press. The figures for paid distribution in 1977 come from the OJD and *Expansion*, April, 1979.

Italy, the cradle of the photo-novel, consumes two million and one million copies weekly of *Intimita* and *Grand Hotel* respectively. By comparison, the best-selling fashion magazine attains only a quarter of this volume. In France, *Nous Deux* and *Intimité*, closely linked with its Italian namesake, have weekly sales of 985,000 and 715,000 respectively. The statistics also show the sudden fall of the illustrious *Elle* and *Marie-Claire*. The sales figures for *Marie-Claire* have fallen by half over the last fifteen years. From a million copies in 1960, it dropped to half a million in 1975. At the same time, *Elle* fell from 650,000 copies in 1960 to 400,000 in 1975. Yet, between 1968 and 1975, the photo-novel magazine *Intimité* saw its sales rise by thirty per cent.

Who reads this type of magazine? In Italy, those under thirty-five constitute fifty-seven per cent of the readership of *Grand Hotel*. In France, forty-seven per cent of the readers of *Nous Deux* and *Intimité* come from the same age group. Forty-eight per cent of the readership of *Nous Deux* has as its head of family a skilled or unskilled worker or foreman, fourteen per cent an employee or clerk and twenty-three per cent are unemployed or students. Sources: *Tarif Media*, November and December, 1976, and the reports of *Presse Actualités*.

8. "Discurso a las mujeres", *El Mercurio*, 25 April, 1974.
9. *El Mercurio*, 26 June, 1974.
10. *El Mercurio*, 12 May, 1975.
11. "The slogan, *emancipation of women*, has its roots only in Jewish intellectualism. The German woman in the truly palmy days of German life has no need for emancipation any more than in those same good days need the man fear that he may be wrenched out of his place by woman. Only when there was a lack of absolute certainty in the knowledge of her task did the eternal instinct of self and race preservation begin to revolt in woman, then there grew from this revolt a state of affairs that was unnatural and which lasted until both sexes returned to the respective spheres which an eternally wise Providence has pre-ordained for them." Hitler's speech to the Women's Congress at Nüremberg, September, 1934. Quoted in Robert A. Brady, *The Spirit and Structure of German Fascism*, Left Book Club Edition, Victor Gollancz, London, 1937, p. 188.

Other titles from Comedia

Organizations and Democracy Series